WAIKIKI

IN THE WAKE OF DREAMS

This book is the companion project of
WAIKIKI, In The Wake of Dreams,
the documentary film
Copyright © Paul Berry and Edgy Lee
Sponsored by
The Pacific Arts Foundation Inc.

Library of Congress Card Number: 00-104888

ISBN 0-9701014-0-6

Written by Paul Berry & Edgy Lee
Edited by Nina Berry &
MacKinnon Simpson
Designed by Michel V.M. Lê

Printed in China through Colorcraft Ltd, Hong Kong

First Hard Cover Edition
May 2000

 **First Hawaiian Bank** made this book possible through its generous assistance

4

The assistance and guidance

of many generous, thoughtful

people have made this book

possible. The authors are

deeply grateful for their art,

stories, thoughts, knowledge,

kindness, encouragement, and

talented contributions. Our

thanks go to:

First
Hawaiian
Bank

IN ASSOCIATION WITH SPONSORING ORGANIZATIONS & BUSINESSES:

ABC
STORES

DFS GALLERIA

Wimberly Allison Tong & Goo
Architects, Planners and Consultants

honu
GROUP INC

Bishop Museum
Funded through a Cooperative Agreement with
The National Park Service U.S. Dept. of the Interior

And
WAIKIKI, IN THE WAKE OF DREAMS sponsored by:

HAWAI'I VISITORS & CONVENTION BUREAU ~ O'AHU VISITORS BUREAU, in association with

THE QUEEN EMMA FOUNDATION ~ MATSON NAVIGATION COMPANY ~ ALOHA AIRLINES (*and* HUNG WO & ELIZABETH CHING FOUNDATION)

SHERATON HOTELS IN WAIKIKI *and* THE LUXURY COLLECTION HAWAI'I

ABC STORES

HISTORICAL & PHOTOGRAPHIC RESOURCES:
**Bishop Museum Native Hawaiian Culture &
Arts Program**: *Special mahalo to Dr. Donald
Duckworth, Pat Duarte, Dr. Betty Tatar, Betty
Kam, David Kemble, Nancy Young, DeSoto Brown,
Marge White*
Honolulu Magazine ~ Paradise of the Pacific:
David Pellegrin, Chairman; John Alves, Publisher;
John Heckathorn, Editor
Hawai'i State Archives
**The University of Hawai'i at Manoa ~ Center
for Oral History**: Warren & Michi Nishimoto
The Honolulu Academy of Arts: Dr. George
Ellis, Jennifer Seville, Charlie Aldinger, Pauline
Sugino
Peabody Museum: Salem, Massachusetts
Hawai'i State Judiciary Center
Dr. John Cox & The L.J. Crampon Collection
R.M. Towill Corporation

The Hawaii Visitors & Convention Bureau:
*Special mahalo to Tony Vericella, Les Enderton,
Gail Ann Chew, Darlene Morikawa, Kathleen Lau*
Hawaiian Historical Society
Mission Houses Museum
Mary Judd & the Hue Luquiens Collection
Matson Navigation Company: R.J. Pfeiffer,
C. Bradley Mulholland, Paul Stevens, Bal Dreyfus,
Gary Nakamatsu, Anita Denz, Yvette Ho
Editions Ltd.: Gaylord Wilcox, Grady Timmons
Hawai'i Maritime Center
FilmWorks Ltd.
Jacket was inspired by 1915 Mid-Pacific Carnival
poster design.
SPECIAL MAHALO TO:
Walter A. Dods Jr., John K. Tsui, Anthony R.
Guerrero Jr., Lily Yao, Brandt Farias, City &
County of Honolulu & Mayor Jeremy Harris,
Robert Oshiro, Barry Okuda, Sonny Ching, Pinky
Ching, Keith Vierra, John Votsis, Paul Kosasa,

Sue & Gordon Damon, Atherton Foundation,
Waikiki Improvement Association, Rick Egged,
Network Media, McInerny Ltd., Hawaiian Tug &
Barge, Coca Cola Bottling Hawaii, E Noa Tours,
Sally Kim, Mary Baker, Robert Oshiro, Barry
Okuda, Rosemary Fazio, and David Farmer
WRITERS & EDITORS:
MacKinnon Simpson, Grady Timmons,
Will Kyselka, Nina Berry
PHOTOGRAPHERS & ARTISTS:
Olivier Koning, Herb Kawainui Kane, Duane
Preble, Nip Akona, Michel V.M. Lê, James Wellner
CONSULTANTS, INTERVIEWEES, HISTORIANS & FRIENDS:
Waikiki Aquarium, The Friends of Iolani Palace,
Harry Robello, U.S. Senator Daniel K. Inouye,
Boyce Rodrigues, Larry Mehau, Robert J. Pfeiffer,
Don Ho, Dr. George Kanahele, Puakea Nogelmeier,
Kumu Hula Sonny Ching & Halau Na Mamo O

Puuanahulu, Dr. Richard Rapson, Dr. Duane
Preble, Haumea Heibenstreit, Tom Moffatt, Pam
Anderson, Heidi Berman, Benny Kalama, David
Uchiyama, Cynthia Rankin, Erica MacGuyer, The
Royal Hawaiian, Moana Hotel, Cobey Black,
Wayne Harada, Eddie Sherman, Sam Kapu, Bob
Krauss, Kamaka Clark Miyamoto, Kalu
Cummings, Jerry Byrd, Arthur Lyman, New Otani
Kaimana Hotel, Fred Hemmings, the Family of
Wong Kwai, Marilyn Stassen-McLaughlin, Christie
Weaver, Family of Sam Nainoa, Family of
Steamboat Mokuahi, Family of Vicky Fi
Rodrigues, George Winston, Don Ho's Island Grill,
Brew Moon, Todd Lawrence, Shawn Rubert,
Helen & Edwin K.W. Lee, Barbara & Judge
Tenney Tongg, Joanne Shigekane, Capt. David
Lyman, Peter Rotsel, Michael P. Foley, John &
Heidi Marciel-Vavul, Daniel Chung, Helena Chow,
Vicky Fong, Christine & Charlotte Lê, Cheryl
Cole, Oscar deWilde

WAIKIKI
IN THE WAKE OF DREAMS

WRITTEN BY PAUL BERRY & EDGY LEE

EDITED BY NINA BERRY & MACKINNON SIMPSON

DESIGNED BY MICHEL V.M. LÊ

PUBLISHED BY

FILMWORKS PRESS

WAIKIKI
IN THE WAKE OF DREAMS

Men in Fruitladen Canoe by Arman T. Manookian Collection of Mr. and Mrs. C.F. Damon, Jr.

FOREWORD

In years following the arrival of western explorers on Hawai'i's shores, various Hawaiian kings battled for control of O'ahu, and particularly its crown jewel, Waikiki. As the 21st century begins, Waikiki is once more at the center of a controversy, but this time differences are focused on what Waikiki has become, and what it ought to be. We hope this book will pass along a sense of the people and stories that form the history of this remarkable place.

Perhaps with a better understanding of her past, residents and visitors who will come to write the next chapters of Waikiki's future will add something of their own to this unfinished story.

Paul Berry and Edgy Lee

12

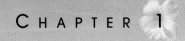

Magic Beside the Sea

People who like this sort of thing will find this the sort of thing they like.

From a book review by Abraham Lincoln

We give names to places in order to understand them, to find our way and to tell our stories. So here are the stories behind the names that make up Waikiki, the stories of generations who dreamed and lived the good life, who felt the mysterious pull of this place reminding them of life's possibilities.

In Waikiki the names stretch like the roots of a great banyan tree into the soil of the past. Waikiki itself speaks of "spouting waters," where Hawaiians found fresh water springs to feed their taro patches. Diamond Head reminds us that early British seamen mistook the calcite crystals atop Leʻahi for diamonds. Olohana Street repeats the shout of "All Hands" that American sailor John Young made to his Hawaiian shipmates as they battled to assure Kamehameha's conquest of the islands. Kalakaua, Kaʻiulani, and Kuhio Avenues all take their names from Hawaiians of royal blood. Kalakaua's queen, Kapiʻolani, whose name means "heavenly arch," lends her name to the lovely Park beneath Diamond Head. Ala Wai, meaning "fresh water way," describes the canal created in the 1920's where streams from three valleys flow into Waikiki.

At the beginning of a new century, in Waikiki's timeless dance of palm trees, sky, and sea, you can find a poem, one there to be read every day.

It is written in the curve of sand along the beach, in the fall of sunlight on the hibiscus along Kalakaua Avenue, and in the smiles of Hawaiian kids eager for the energy of Waikiki's waves. In the sweeping views of blue from hotel room balconies, and in the shadows of *kiawe* trees when the moonlight floods Kapi'olani Park, there is a poetry that has no equivalent in words, not even in the names of places. It is something felt rather than understood, the fragrance of leis and ocean air, a quiet sense of waves, people, buildings, and birds on the wing, each part of the rhythm of paradise.

Paradise. The very word speaks of man's oldest dream — blue skies, a friendly breeze, cares gone, an Eden where fantasies become realities, and life smiles.

DIAMOND HEAD

While Hawai'i has hundreds of volcanic landmarks, nature has crafted only one Diamond Head, an imposing shape recognized immediately from Iowa to Istanbul.

This famous signature in stone emerged some 300,000 years ago in a process quite different from the eruptions that send molten lava spouting and flowing from the volcano at Kilauea. In ancient Waikiki, molten rock worked its way up, superheating water into steam trapped in lava tubes and reef rocks just below the surface. Like a pressure cooker with too much energy to be contained, the compressed steam built up, then set off a catastrophic explosion, blasting material out of the crater at a low angle where it formed a circle about a kilometer in diameter.

The force of the explosion spent, the crater's walls slumped, sealing off the vent. With more heat from below and more water turning to steam, pressure built up again and again, creating a series of explosive episodes that added ash and dust to the walls of the crater's perimeter. Rising magma came into contact with water, changed chemically, and fractured into a brownish palgonite that eventually cemented into a semi-solid rock appropriately called tuff. Geologists classify Diamond Head as a tuff cone.

The higher crown on the seaward side, Le'ahi, indicates that trade winds blowing at the time deposited more ash to that edge of the crater, leaving it nearly twice the height of the surrounding rim. Since then, rising seas following the end of an ice age have eroded Diamond Head's walls, making their inclines steeper and exposing beds of tuff at the summit. Embedded there, you'll find carbonized remains of plants, bits of white reef rock, and small chunks of basalt.

The volcanic origin of Diamond Head sometimes leaves people wondering if it will explode again. According to geologists, the answer to that is no, at least not in any era when people will be reading this book.

Will Kyselka

Hawaiians will tell you that Leʻahi was regarded as a sacred mountain. On the Ewa (west) side of the slopes was a *holua* or rock slide which *aliʻi* (royalty) would cover with leaves and mats so they could careen down on sleds! Hawaiians are said to have kept a fire burning atop the crest (*Lae Ahi* = fire headland) to guide travelers from other islands, and later, flagmen would signal Honolulu with the arrival on incoming ships. Hawaiian myth also held that the imposing head of land was named Laeʻahi by Hiʻiaka, sister of the goddess Pele, while she was passing from Kauaʻi. *Lae-ahi*, the brow of an *ahi* or tuna, shortened in time into Leʻahi. [1]

During the Spanish-American War, soldiers camped for several years in an area of Kapiʻolani Park, labeling it Camp McKinley, after the president. Apparently they admired Diamond Head so much that in 1904, the U.S. military bought 729 acres and over the years fortified it with artillery, tunnels and bunkers for ammunition and personnel. After World War II, its large concrete underground spaces became the air traffic control center for the entire mid-Pacific. [2]

In the late 1960's Diamond Head was besieged by short-sighted developers proposing to adorn its slopes with high-rise hotels, but the fabled landmark was saved when legions of outraged residents persuaded local government to stop such folly. Today many Waikiki visitors hike or drive through the tunnel into the crater, then climb hundreds of steps on the path to the peak for a magnificent view of Honolulu and the sea.

Mounted on a large rock in Kapiʻolani Park, you'll find the following plaque:

DIAMOND HEAD
Has Been Designated A Registered Natural Landmark.
This site possesses exceptional value in illustrating
the natural history of the United States.

U.S. Department of Interior National Park Service, 1968.

Lily Pond and Coconut Grove, Waikiki by H.W. Kelley, Courtesy Bishop Museum

18

Chapter 2

Ancient Waikiki

Let others praise the ancient times; I am glad I was born in these.
Ovid, 43 BC -- 18 CE

Where timeless waves sweep toward a golden shore, there are stories told, and those who tell them. Stories of how water works its magic on all who come, stories of conquerors and queens . . . of trade winds casting wondrous spells . . . of sightseers and sand castles . . . midnight revolutionaries and healers . . . beachboys and poets . . . all drawn by the beauty of this distant island and this special place — Waikiki.

A tropic moon, the melody of an *'ukulele*, the roll of surf. For over two centuries people have brought their dreams to this shore. And if by some magic Waikiki could talk, imagine the stories she would tell.

Born in fire, O'ahu emerged perhaps 3.8 million years ago and ever so slowly edged northwest some 140 miles from its point of origin. As if sculpted by the hands of wind and sea, Diamond Head took the shape of an ancient Polynesian Sphinx, guardian of the natural beauty below. Then, in just the last tick of the geological clock, the Polynesians came.

Discovery of Oahu by Herb Kawainui Kane — Collection of The Outrigger Waikiki Hotel ~ Courtesy of the Artist

WAIKIKI

From its earliest days it was a place where the human spirit could rest and heal from a busy world. Fed by three streams from the majestic Koʻolau Mountains, this vast *ahupuaʻa*, a wedge of land running from mountains to sea, formed a natural marshland and breadbasket for early Hawaiians — *loʻi* terraces for taro, fishponds, fine fishing off-shore, and fresh water springs to irrigate the crops as well. Ponds and marshlands stretched from below Diamond Head to the slopes of Makiki Heights, and Hawaiians felt this meeting of fresh and sea water created not just a gathering place, but a place of great healing powers, great spirit or *mana*.

The combination of beauty, food from sea and land, a delightful climate, and its history as a spiritual center led the legendary reigning chief Maʻilikukahi to make Waikiki the capital of Oʻahu from the 15th century on. [1]

A subsequent chief, Kahuhelewa, had his people plant coconuts at Helumoa, creating a royal grove of ten thousand coconut trees. In a chant dating to that era, a man named Kawelo sang of his love for the place and for a woman he met there, an early record of Waikiki's enchanting beauty. [2]

The power of this solitary shore to fire the imagination and dreams of romance would repeat often in the stories of kings, commoners, and the countless visitors who followed.

NA POHAKU

They sit there silent as of old, and though the largest weighs some seven and a half tons, the ancient healing stones, *Na Pohaku Ola Ulukou*, attract more pigeons than passersby. Perhaps 1,000 years ago healers arrived by canoe from Raiataea. Under their spiritual guidance, thousands of Hawaiians moved these same stones from distant Kaimuki, to place them and their healing powers here by the spouting waters of Waikiki. [3] Legend holds that these *pohaku* (stones) were used with prayers and incantations to work miraculous cures.

The presence of several *heʻiau* (Hawaiian stone platform temples) in Waikiki adds to its history as a place for spiritual practice. Two *heʻiau* were situated at Helumoa (site of the present Royal Hawaiian Hotel) and Ulukou, (site of the present Moana Hotel). Helumoa's use dates to 1610, when an upstart Maui chief invaded Oʻahu, and lost both the battle and his life there. [4]

NOT EXACTLY PARADISE

The catalogue of trouble around 1800 shows that it would have been the wrong time to vacation in Waikiki. Over the centuries intermittent wars had interrupted the tranquillity, but now sailing ships, cannons, and deadly firearms stirred ambitious dreams in some of Hawai'i's chiefs, leaving the islands a sometimes risky place for visiting sailors. A British merchant captain named William Brown discovered Honolulu Harbor in 1793, but Hawaiians who wanted his armaments and ship killed him. Between 1780 and 1795, chiefs from outer islands took turns invading O'ahu, their battles eventually leaving forces there unable to repel outsiders.

WINDS OF CHANGE

The islands of the Hawaiian chain are the most remote landform on Earth, and their original discovery remains a mystery at which navigators can only wonder. Polynesians found Hawai'i and navigated back and forth to Tahiti long centuries before westerners reached the Pacific. Just which western sailor first came upon them remains something of a puzzle.

Spanish archives indicate that 223 years before Cook arrived, a Spanish Captain named Gaetano found the islands and named them La Major, La Mesa, and La Desgraciada. [5] Other clues also suggest early landings in Hawai'i: "many iron utensils" found on Kaua'i by Captain Clerke, part of Cook's expedition; a 17th century Dutch globe showing islands near the location of Hawai'i; and stories that early visitors heard older Hawaiians tell of foreigners cast up on the island of Hawai'i. [6]

The missionary William Ellis cites that in 1823 Hawaiians had two accounts of white visitors prior to Cook, one of these stories telling of seven white people landing at Kealakekua Bay, intermarrying, and living out their lives as chiefs on the island of Hawai'i. [7]

In 1778-79, Cook found and charted the coordinates of what he called the Sandwich Islands (in honor of his patron). With publication of Cook's discovery, powerful strangers began to arrive in tall ships, and with them came unimaginable changes — guns . . . cattle . . . alcohol . . . diseases.

Captain James Cook's Pacific expeditions were voyages of discovery. When his ships returned to London, the carefully kept journals and meticulously drawn maps were published, opening the world for trade and future exploration.

CAPITAL OF THE KINGDOM

In 1795 Kamehameha the Great and his army of 10,000 warriors arrived on Oʻahu, beaching some 1200 war canoes along the shores of Waikiki. Conquest came quickly, as Kamehameha's men fought skirmishes across the marshes and plains, and in a decisive battle in Nuʻuanu Valley, conquered the island of Oʻahu. It took Kamehameha's troops months to find his opponent Kalanikupule (hiding in Ewa) and return him to Waikiki, where he met his demise.

Waikiki worked its magic on the conqueror. The shelter of Diamond Head made the waters offshore a smooth anchorage for visiting vessels, and Kamehameha settled for a few years at the mouth of ʻApuakehau stream, which ran to the sea in Waikiki. There he built a stone house, and lived with his wife Keopuolani. Two of their sons would become the next two kings of Hawaiʻi. [8]

On the winds of change came merchant ships and more explorers, and with them trouble — an interest in foreign finery, the use of credit and money, and the influence of foreign customs. Worse, visitors brought diseases, and some Hawaiian women married foreigners, after noting that children of mixed blood had higher survival rates. Although he fell ill, Kamehameha survived the *mai okuʻu*, (cholera or bubonic plague), which ravaged Waikiki and killed nearly half the population of the island in 1804. Diamond

Head became a burial site for some of the victims of this epidemic, which left Waikiki's taro fields short of men to work them. [9]

Despite the losses, Hawaiians in Waikiki and Honolulu continued their traditional entertainments and sports: kite flying (huge kites made of tapa/mulberry cloth), surfing, boxing, wrestling, a bowling game using a traditional two pound round stone (*ulu maika*), foot races, and perhaps most useful of all, spear-dodging. Kamehameha himself was a legendary spear dodger. Sporting events of this era drew thousands of spectators, some of them gamblers who would visit the homes of contestants before the contest to check the athletes' physical conditioning, then bet — tools, livestock, even homes — on the outcome. Observers described the losers as raging over their losses. [10]

On their way to China from the Pacific Northwest, western trading vessels would stop for provisions off Waikiki. Soon Hawaiʻi's beautiful and fragrant *ʻiliahi* (sandalwood) replaced sea otter pelts in a brisk trade with the Far East.

While Waikiki remained Oʻahu's breadbasket with its taro and superb fishing, Kamehameha moved his capital to Honolulu Harbor in 1808 to accommodate the arrival of large trading ships. His own royal fleet remained in Waikiki. Kamehameha himself worked Waikiki's fields, cleared land for taro, went deep sea fishing off Waikiki, surfed there into his elder years, and was much admired because he ensured that everyone shared in the abundance. [11]

Newcomers added exotic forms of food, lodging, and recreation. In 1809 Don Francisco Paula de Marin imported a variety of Mexican California's wonders, including lemons, figs, tamarind trees, grapes, and pineapple.

A retrospective of Honolulu Harbor in 1850, painted by Peter Hurd in honor of Amfac's 100th Anniversary in 1949.

WHALERS, MISSIONARIES, AND UNCERTAIN TIMES

As merchants, whalers, and missionaries began to arrive in Hawai'i in the first quarter of the 19th century, Waikiki remained a quiet farming community with a fine beach, a place loved by Hawai'i's *ali'i* (royalty). When John Whitman visited in 1813 he found that, "At Whyteetee there is a forest of cocoa nut trees covering a number of acres, we used to enjoy the cool of the day, in playing ball and other recreation." [12] But just down the beach, trouble was brewing, or more exactly, distilling. "Some Botany Bay (Australia) convicts, having made their escape to O'ahu, were received into the service of the king (Kamehameha the Great) and small allotments of land given them. On them they raised sugar cane and contrived a still to manufacture ardent spirits. They produced the usual results — neglect of work, riots, and quarrels." [13] At Kewalo, next to what is now Ala Moana Park, a fellow named Oliver Holmes set up the first rum distillery, and soon the great Kamehameha had one installed for himself. His experiences with demon rum, however, later led him to give up on alcohol entirely. Regardless, drink began to pose serious problems for the Hawaiian kingdom. [14]

Honolulu Harbor scene in the late 1800's.

25

The death of Kamehameha the Great in 1819 left Hawai'i without its unifying force, and several decades of wild, turbulent times followed. Ancient religious and social *kapu* (taboos) of Hawaiian culture were soon broken, and with a king too young to rule effectively, rumors of an overthrow came and went. With tens, then hundreds of whaling ships stopping twice a year for provisions, demand for salt beef soared. Ranches began to appear throughout the islands, and *paniolo* (Hawaiian cowboys) rode the range.

Newly arrived missionaries insisted on changes in the dress and behavior of Hawaiians, and mysterious epidemics devastated the population. And as you might expect, hard drinking sailors and teetotaling missionaries found little to agree on.

As *ali'i* piled up debts for their purchases of fancy foreign goods, the United States in 1826 sent a warship, the *U.S.S. Dolphin*, to help enforce collections for American merchants. Regent Ka'ahumanu was trying to curtail drinking and outlaw prostitution at the time, but the captain of the *Dolphin* threatened to shell Honolulu unless his men were allowed access to Hawaiian women. His sailors joined those from other vessels in a riot, delivering an ultimatum that they be allowed prostitutes. [15] Given the demands of this kind of rough visitor trade, it comes as no surprise that the number of taverns was increasing in direct proportion to the arrival of thirsty sailors.

A LAW REGULATING THE SALE OF ARDENT SPIRITS.

Whereas we have seen that drinking of ardent spirits and other intoxicating liquors is of great injury to our country; therefore I with my chiefs have sought for the means of suppressing it.

1st We prohibit all selling of spirits by any person whatsoever, either openly or secretly, without written license. Whoever is detected selling, or doing contrary to this law, shall be fined fifty dollars, and if he sell again he shall be fined one hundred dollars; thus shall the fine be increased by the addition of fifty dollars for every repetition of the offence, to the utmost violation of this law.

2. If however any person, whether foreigner or native, sell spirits by the barrel or large cask, he will not be amenable to this law, but any person who sells in any smaller quantity, will be liable to its penalty.

3. Any house having been lisenced for retailing spirits, may sell by the glass, but not by any larger measure; and its doors must be closed by ten o'clock at night, and all visitors must go away until morning. And on Sunday such house shall not be opened from ten o'clock on Saturday night until Monday morning.

4. We prohibit drunkenness in the licensed houses. If any one whether foreigner or native, drink and become drunk at such house, the owner of the house where he got drunk shall pay the following fine. Ten dollars for the first offence, twenty dollars for the second, and thus the fine will be increased by the addition of ten dollars for every repetition, to the extent of his misdemeanors.

5. The officers appointed to this duty will watch, and they will quietly observe whatever in going on in the said houses. Let no one obstruct them in their duty.

6. Any house licensed for selling spirits, and conducting in a manner at variance with this law, will, on conviction, have its license taken away and it will not be given back again.

KAMEHAMEHA III.
LAHAINA March 20 1838.

Right: Anthony Allen, who had escaped slavery in the United States, found Hawai'i a place to prosper and raise his family. He established a boarding house, a bowling alley, a saloon, and a small hospital on the Waikiki plain, two miles east of the village of Honolulu near what we now know as Pawa'a. [16]

Wally Amos plays Anthony D. Allen, in the documentary film, *Waikiki, In the Wake of Dreams.*

In his *Journal*, C.S. Stewart describes Anthony D. Allen:

"He is quite a respectable man; and has a very neat establishment, consisting of a dozen houses built in the native manner, and covered with mud; one for sitting and sleeping, one for eating, another for a storehouse, another for milk, a kitchen, a blacksmith's shop, etc. He also keeps a kind of boarding house for seamen . . . His plantation is two miles from Mission House on the plain, towards Waititi. The road to it, although the plain is uncultivated and entirely unshaded, affords the most pleasant walk." [17]

THE SPERM WHALE "IN A FLURRY."

LITH. & PUB. BY N. CURRIER.

Entered according to Act of Congress in the year 1852 by N. Currier, in the Clerk's Office of the District Court of the Southern District of N.Y.

152 NASSAU STREET, N.Y.

Whaling in 1880

Others saw the commercial possibilities of Waikiki early as well, for 19th century Hawaiian historian Samuel Kamakau records a tavern in the coconut grove at Kalia (inland from of today's Waikiki Yacht Harbor), owned by an Englishman named James C. Lyman. [18]

When Kaʻahumanu finally set out in 1828 to close all the taverns, an angry crowd of Hawaiians, sailors, and tavern keepers assembled in Waikiki on the beach at Helumoa, bent on killing the Christian chiefs and forcing American missionaries to go elsewhere. If a respected high chief named Kekuanaoʻa and the missionary Hiram Bingham had not talked them out of it, the history of Waikiki and Hawaiʻi itself would probably have unfolded very differently. [19]

When Kaʻahumanu died in 1832, the floodgates opened again for drinking, prostitution, and gambling, only to close and open several more times as the king, merchants, missionaries, sea captains, and tavern keepers vied over how to meet the demands of the visitor trade yet still keep public order. [20]

The most celebrated sex scandal of the era played out like a modern soap opera. Kamanawa, a high chief and grandfather of a child who later would become king (Kalakaua), wanted to marry a woman he had fallen for. Inconveniently, he was already married and couldn't get a divorce. After he and an accomplice poisoned his wife, the two were caught and hanged before a crowd of 10,000 on October 20, 1840. [21]

By 1837 John Mitchener and F.W. Thompson established a tavern, boarding house, and bowling alley, which they advertised in the new English language paper called the *Sandwich Islands Gazette and Journal of Commerce* as the Hotel Waikiki.

HOTEL WAITITI.

JOHN MITCHENER,

ever grateful for the past liberal patronage already bestowed upon him by his friends and the public, would respectfully inform, that he has opened a

HOTEL at WAITITI.

Including a **BOWLING ALLEY** and other such facilities for amusement and recreation as to add to the comfort of gentlemen who honor him by their visits.

Horses and Carriages will be carefully attended by his servants.

THE BAR will be constantly furnished with the best wines and liquors; **HIS TABLE** will be supplied at the shortest notice with the choicest viands.

Gentlemen alone, or parties will receive constant attention from MR. MITCHENER, and his assistant MR. MELLISH, and short notice will ensure the most extensive arrangements required for the gratification of visitors.

JOHN MITCHENER

hopes to receive the patronage of the public at the NEW HOTEL." [22]

Mitchener prospered and sold nine years later to one John Freeman, after whom the history of this first Waikiki hotel vanishes. Another hotel in Waikiki's grove of coconut trees would not appear for half a century. [23]

COMMENTARIES OF THE TIMES

Beyond the trouble clouding the times, Hawaiians enjoyed some material and cultural benefits brought from the outside world. From visitors Hawaiians quickly learned metalsmithing, ship building, carpentry, plumbing, bricklaying, horsemanship, literacy, and printing. Vaqueros from Mexico taught Hawaiians how to round up cattle, and perhaps most important of all, they brought with them new forms of music — guitars, songs, and singing styles from Spain, Mexico, and South America. Visiting concert musicians and opera divas entertained. During the reign of the music-loving young Kamehameha III, the King's Band (later called the Royal Hawaiian Band), under the leadership of a freed African-American slave named Oliver, greeted major foreign visitors. Oliver was later replaced as Royal Hawaiian bandmaster by George Washington Hyatt, another former slave who also found his way to Hawai'i.

Although European and American influences had in many ways westernized religion, farming, and trade, the Hawaiian way of life in this era still had its share of foreign commentators and new arrivals who wondered at native life.

"The pets of nobles, of whatever kind, have in many cases uncontrollable privileges. There is at present attached to the palace a hog of this character, weighing four or five hundred pounds, called 'Kaahumanu' after the haughty dowager of that name, which is permitted to range at pleasure, within doors as without; and not infrequently finds a bed among the satins and silks of the royal couches"

C. S. Stewart, *Journal of a Residence in The Sandwich Islands* [24]

"Canoes of naked natives are alongside our vessel and coming on board. O my sisters, you cannot tell how the sight of these poor degraded creatures, both literally and spiritually naked, would affect you!"

Missionary's wife, Sybil Bingham, upon her arrival in 1820 [25]

"*By invitation of Mr. Douglass, I took a ride with the young chiefs. We rode to Waititi where there is fine bathing in the surf... Near the beach are fine groves of cocoanut trees, several thatched houses, one of which is occupied as a dressing apartment.*

The young Chiefs are all provided with surf boards...12 to 20 feet long, 1 ft. wide, and in the middle 5 or 6 inches thick, thinning off towards the sides and ends so as to form an edge. None belonging to Kamehameha the First are now left, but one used by Kaahumanu and other chiefs are daily used by the boys... Some have been handed down in the royal family for years, as this is the royal bathing place."

C. S. Lyman, *The Hawaiian Journals of Chester Smith Lyman* [26]

CHAPTER 3

Shaping the Dream: 1848-1901

Kūlia i ka nuʻu. Strive to reach the highest.

Motto of Queen Kapiʻolani

Alive in the midst of it, few among us have much sense of the flow of history that carries us along. Even if you had owned a crystal ball in mid-19th century Hawai'i, you could not have predicted how events thousands of miles away would soon reshape island life. California's new independence from Mexico and the discovery of gold above Sacramento sent mainland trade with Hawai'i soaring. And when someone discovered petroleum in Pennsylvania in 1859, it took just over a decade for whaling to disappear. The visitor trade with sailors and sales of Hawaiian beef to whaling ships faded, then vanished. While island entrepreneurs cast about for new ways to make money, the American Civil War some five thousand miles away cut off sugar sales from America's southern to northern states. Hawai'i's Great Land Division of 1848 made it possible for foreigners to buy land, and now they did, expanding sugar production tenfold, and importing contract laborers from China, Portugal, and later Japan to work the cane. Who would have predicted the export of sugar and later pineapple would profoundly alter Hawai'i's population mix, or that parts of Waikiki would become a rice bowl and Waikiki itself transform into a world famous attraction for visitors.

Mark Twain as a young man.

Waikiki's fate now tied more closely to what happened in the urban center near the harbor and elsewhere on O'ahu. Epidemics cost Waikiki many of its Hawaiian taro farmers, and Chinese farmers began to replace them, replanting parts of Waikiki with rice. When the importation of Chinese sugar workers in 1852 began to create demand, Waikiki supplied rice to feed immigrant workers.

In the 1860's commerce between California and Hawai'i was so active that the *Sacramento Union* sent a young writer named Samuel Clemens (aka Mark Twain) to report on the wonders of paradise. Twain proved a keen observer of O'ahu's visitor trade. He wrote:

"Sailors always spend all their money before they leave port. Last year they spent $150,000 here. In the palmy days of whaling, 20 years ago, they squandered as high as a million and a half in this port at the end of a successful voyage. [1]

"Rest assured that tremendous trade is to spring up between California and the Islands the next few years ... Hawai'i is (now) too far away ... 20 days to come here and 30 to get back in a sailing vessel. But if California can send capitalists down here in seven days and take them back in ten she can fill these islands full of Americans." [2]

In fact, despite the drop off in provisioning whaling ships, it was still common for a hundred and fifty merchant vessels to call in the islands during the mid-1860's. Hawai'i had for two generations relied on income from visitors, and now it moved strongly toward the export of sugar.

Downtown Honolulu now boasted a brand new luxury hotel, the elaborate Royal, which visitors loved. The kingdom financed the hotel, which was a preview of the Royal that would appear in Waikiki half a century later. World traveler Isabella Bird saw it this way:

> *"This is the perfection of a hotel. Hospitality seems to take possession of one as soon as one enters its never-closed doors. A place pervaded by kindliness. One can sit all day on the verandah watching the play of light and color on the mountains and the deep blue green of the valley.*
>
> *Wide corridors are lively with English and American naval uniforms, several planters' families are here for the season; health seekers from California, resident boarders, whaling captains, tourists from the British Pacific Colonies, and a stream of townspeople . . . Life here is truer, simpler, happier than ours.* [3]

THE ROYAL · HAWAIIAN HOTEL,

W. M. GRAHAM, MANAGER.

TERMS, $3. PER DAY. - - - - - $75 PER MOTNH

This Hotel is one of the leading architectural structures of Honolulu. The grounds upon which it stands comprise an entire square of about four acres, fronting on Hotel street. This large area affords ample room for a lawn and beautiful walks, which are laid out most artistically with flowering plants and tropical trees. There are twelve pretty cottages within this charming enclosure, all under the Hotel management. The Hotel and cottages afford accommodations for two hundred guests. The basement of the Hotel contains the Finest Billiard Hall in the City.

The main entrance is on the ground floor, to the right of which are Elegantly Furnished Parlors. A broad passage-way leads from the main hall to the dining-room. These apartments open on broad verandas, where a Magnificent View of the Nuuanu Mountains may be seen through the wealth of tropical foliage that surrounds the balconies. The Fare dispensed is the Best the Market Affords, and is First-Class in all respects. Hotel and cottages are supplied with Pure Water from an Artesian Well on the premises. The Clerk's Office is furnished with the Telephone, by which communication is had with the Leading Business Firms of the City.

Every effort has been made, and money lavishly expended, under the present able management, to make this Establishment THE MODEL FAMILY HOTEL, a reputation it now enjoys and most justly merits.

With his gifts for embellishment, Twain described the creatures that visitors encountered in the Honolulu of the era:

> *"If you get into conversation with a stranger in Honolulu, it is a safe bet that he is either a missionary or captain of a whaler ... one half of the population. I am now personally acquainted with 72 captains and 96 missionaries . . .* [4] *And cats — Tom cats, longtailed cats, bobtail cats, blind cats, one eyed cats, wall eyed cats, cross eyed cats, gray, black, white, yellow striped cats, tame cats, wild cats, individual cats, groups of cats, platoons of cats, companies of cats, regiments of cats, armies of cats, millions of cats, and all of them sleek, fat, lazy, and sound asleep.* [5]

Hideaway Waikiki began to change in 1865, when a road eased travel there from Honolulu. Hawaiian royalty kept Waikiki beach cottages, and wealthy *kama'aina* families began to add their own structures to create a colony. They were simple one-story houses amid many grass shacks.

Twain reached Waikiki and reported:

"A mile and a half from town. I came to a grove of tall coconut trees reaching straight up sixty feet, topped with a spray of green foliage sheltering clusters of coconuts — a forest of colossal ragged parasols with bunches of magnified grapes under them. The grass cabins are of a grayish color . . . and are made of some kind of weed bound strongly together . . . His Majesty . . . owns the whole concern and passes his time there frequently, on sultry days "laying off." The spot is called the King's Grove.

The little collection of cottages under the trees is a historical village, Waikiki, once the capital of the kingdom . . . There is an opening in the coral reef at this point, and anchorage . . . Nearby is an interesting ruin — where human sacrifices were offered. The simple child of nature, the luckless sinner, could achieve periodical happiness, . . . long before the missionaries braved to come and make them permanently miserable by telling them how beautiful and blissful heaven is and how nearly impossible it is to get there . . ." [6]

Twain was not prepared for what he discovered during his horseback ride to Diamond Head, where, after evening descended, he and his companions encountered, "a place where no grass grew — a wide expanse of deep sand. All around everywhere, not three feet apart, the bleached bones of men gleamed white in the moonlight . . . All sorts of bones could be found except skulls . . . Many believe this spot to be an ancient battleground . . . and many now believe that these bones belong to victims of one of those epidemics who were hastily buried in a great pit." [7]

Its ossuary aside, Waikiki was still a place of languorous days and nights away from the demands and intrusions of busy Honolulu, a place of abundant fish, and taro. Visitors to Honolulu, however, would also encounter clouds of mosquitoes, numerous rats, no sewers, and an abundance of drunks. The smell of decaying hides drying in the back yard of local merchants wafted *mauka* from the slaughterhouses along Skinner's Wharf, and mingled with the smell of carcasses and human waste. Although connected to Honolulu now by a road and a bridge, Waikiki had avoided the afflictions that commerce had brought to Honolulu.

Twain's Letters found a wide audience, and long years later, he would say that the people and the beauty of Hawai'i still deeply affected him.

"These natives . . . They are amazingly unselfish and hospitable . . . The example of white selfishness does not affect their native unselfishness . . .

"The Sandwich Islands, the peacefullest, restfullest, sunniest, balmiest, dreamiest . . . refuge for a worn and weary spirit the surface of the earth can offer." [8]

TEMPERANCE IN OLD HAWAI'I

Isabella Bird's report from 1873 shows that Hawai'i's kingdom struggled over what to do with alcohol and drugs, a legacy of the near rebellion that stirred on Waikiki Beach back in 1828. In the 1870's, saloon keepers paid a thousand dollars a year for a license, opium was available to any and all, *awa* (a powerful drink made of *awa* root, used throughout the Pacific) was available by medical prescription, and the sale of liquor to native Hawaiians was prohibited. [9]

Bird wrote,

"The islands are large importers. The value of imported goods was $1,184,054 in 1875, on which the Hawaiian Treasury received $213,285 as customs duties. Forty-seven thousand dollars worth of ale, porter, cider, and light wines, and forty-nine thousand dollars worth of spirits, show that the foreign population is more than sufficiently bibulous . . . Twenty-one thousand gallons of spirits were taken out of bond for consumption in 1875. The licenses to sell spirits brought $18,000 into the Treasury in the last biennial period, but those of the sale of awa and opium brought in $55,000 at the same time." [10]

Prior to becoming king, David Kalakaua had called on the legislature to end the hypocrisy of denying Hawaiians drink. [11] Drinking habits changed for many reasons — whaling's rise and fall, epidemics, and the influx of imported foreign laborers — but none seems to explain the vast swings in the commerce of thirst.

GALLONS OF SPIRITS CONSUMED IN HAWAI'I, 1847-1898 (IMPORTED SPIRITS ONLY)				
YEAR	BY RESIDENTS	BY VISITORS	TOTAL	HAWAI'I'S ESTIMATED POPULATION
1847	2,375	896	3,271	87,800
1850	2,777	5,474	8,251	83,900
1853	3,179	15,024	18,203	76,400
1855	3,503	15,025	18,528	72,900
1860	4,297	9,998	14,295	70,200
1865	5,627	6,118	11,745	64,600
1870	7,554	12,394	19,948	59,100
1875	9,208	11,923	21,131	54,200
1880	-	-	44,289	60,400
1885	-	-	80,115	82,000
1890	-	-	88,884	88,700
1895	-	-	39,653	102,000
1898			63,253	120,000

[12]

A RICE BOWL IN WAIKIKI

Hard times continued to trouble Waikiki, diseases now taking the Hawaiian caretakers of Waikiki's royal fishponds, affecting lands the native people had always relied on for food. Hawaiians leased their lands to Chinese rice growers and merchants. "Everybody and his wife is into rice. Taro patches are held at fabulous valuations and among the thoughtful the query is being propounded 'where is our taro to come from?'" [13]

Afong, one of the wealthier Chinese in Hawai'i, married a woman from a Hawaiian family. Wong Kwai, an importer, wholesaler, retailer, and agent for contract labor, converted lands behind Waikiki into rice fields and duck ponds. By 1892, farmers had converted 542 acres of Waikiki to these uses. Inevitably environmental problems followed.

Wong Kwai (bottom right), his #1 wife, sons, and servants, at his mansion in downtown Honolulu.

Graceful old homes:

Although the Land Division of 1848 (Great Mahele) made land title available to all via new western style rules of real estate title, few foreigners owned land in Waikiki during this period.

Kalakaua's sister Likelike and her husband Archibald Cleghorn built *Ainahau*, an Eden within Eden, a beautifully landscaped Waikiki estate boasting an incredible array of plants from all over the world, walkways with bridges, an artesian well, and a grass tennis court. In 1875 Cleghorn planted a banyan tree to commemorate the birth of a daughter, Princess Ka'iulani, the tree maturing into a size that made it legendary. Apuakehau Stream ran through the grounds and exited to the sea, where the present Outrigger Beach Hotel now stands.

Below: Archibald Cleghorn. Right: The James B. Castle Residence, *Kainalu*, circa 1902, designed by architect Oliver G. Traphagen, who also designed the world famous Moana Hotel. Bottom: *Ainahau*, Cleghorn's Estate, circa 1900.

Twain seemed to have a crystal ball regarding which way the winds of politics and trade would now blow:

> *"Americans own the whaling fleet, great sugar plantations; cattle ranches, mercantile depots and lines of packet ships. Consequently, the question of who is to succeed to the crown is an interesting one. The throne has power to help or hinder them a good deal. David Kalakaua is a man of fine presence, an educated gentleman of good abilities. He is politic and calculating, a quiet, dignified, sensible man and would do no discredit to the kingly office."* [14]

Epidemics continued their tragic devastation of the Hawaiian population: measles in 1848; smallpox in 1853; smallpox again in 1881, and the dreaded *mai pake*, leprosy. In an age of rapidly changing technologies and western imperialism, Hawai'i could not afford an army or navy large enough to protect it from powerful imperialist nations. In the 1830's and 1840's a series of incidents with foreign nationals had brought both French and British warships and pressure on the king to accommodate westerners. [15] Now the members of the royal family felt protection of a major power would be a wise international policy. Some favored Britain; others, including David Kalakaua, favored America.

With the monarchy in Hawai'i well established and recognized worldwide, dowager Queen Emma had a close friendship with Queen Victoria and was much loved by the majority of Hawaiians and English residents of the islands. She had extensive holdings in Waikiki, as did other Hawaiian royalty, and acted as hostess for the visiting bachelor Duke of Edinburgh, Queen Victoria's second son. Emma favored Britain as a protector. [16]

ROYAL DAYS ON THE BEACH

Like many of Hawai'i's royalty over the years, Kamehameha IV and Queen Emma spent a lot of time in Waikiki and enjoyed swimming in the ocean. [17] In the early 1870's, Kamehameha V had a beach house at the site of the present Royal Hawaiian Hotel. Chiefs came to Waikiki to swing in the hammock, have parties, surf, and escape the pressures of their positions.

Kamehameha V's beach house

Elected king in 1874, young David Kalakaua had an unusual first task — stopping the riot that started as a result of his election! Ardent followers of Queen Emma sacked the courthouse where the legislature elected him and hospitalized many of those who voted for him. [18]

But the new king soon distinguished himself when he completed a Reciprocity Treaty with the U.S. in 1876, cutting import duties on Hawaiian sugar, and sugar soon dominated the islands' economy.

Kalakaua read in four languages, played several musical instruments, wrote philosophy and authored a book of Hawaiian legends, penned the lyrics to songs, and had a solid knowledge of the classics. He was concerned about Hawai'i's possibilities during an era of western imperialism marching across the Pacific. Early on, he saw the need for Hawai'i to have strong links with Japan. More importantly, he set out to reconstitute Hawaiian culture.

Agnes Quigg wrote,

"During his reign, King Kalakaua actively supported the theme, 'Hawai'i for the Hawaiians,' appointing many Hawaiians to top positions in government, endorsing an act to perpetuate the genealogy of the chiefs, founding a society to revitalize Hawaiian dance, music and art; and encouraging Hawai'i as an international nexus. He was the first monarch to travel around the world, cultivating diplomatic relations among several world powers, and sending envoys to Europe and Asia."

King David Kalakaua

THE KING EYES THE FUTURE

Kalakaua also created a program to educate Hawaiian youths abroad. From 1880 to 1887, young Hawaiians (17 boys, 2 girls) attended schools in six countries where they studied engineering, law, language, medicine, sculpture, music and science. Their descendants include families named Harbottle, Kahanamoku, Paoa, among the few Hawaiians still living in Waikiki when jet travel to the islands began in the 1960's.

One of King Kalakaua's parties.

In the Hawaiian tradition of giving the very best to visitors, Kalakaua entertained lavishly at his exclusive hideaway. The Merry Monarch encouraged artists, reviving Hawaiian music and the hula, a dance destined to later symbolize Waikiki and Hawai'i. He welcomed foreign artists and scholars, and supported the evolution of the Royal Hawaiian Band into a world class musical entity. After visiting Siam and observing a monarch whose indigenous culture retained its identity, the King returned with a renewed desire to preserve native language, dance, chants, and sports.

KAPI'OLANI PARK

Many today hail Kalakaua's next idea as a piece of genius. Working with Archibald Cleghorn, Thomas Cummins, and James Makee, Kalakaua leased lands to a private partnership to create a public park at the base of Diamond Head. Using Cleghorn's design, they planted nearly 10,000 trees, built bridges, walks, and a racetrack, hoping as well to build a casino. Kapi'olani Park became a huge swath of green beauty at the base of Diamond Head, a beautiful centerpiece for O'ahu's people to enjoy.

For a $50 share in the Kapi'olani Park Association, a shareholder had the right to build a house on its perimeter. Cleghorn and Makee introduced peacocks and swans, and Kalakaua's court physician, Dr. George Trousseau, added ostriches — large, aggressive birds — that wandered freely from Kapi'olani Park into Kaimuki. [19]

Above: Kapi'olani Park in 1900, with waterways, ponds and bridges.

Left: Kapi'olani Park today.

STEEL MUSIC

In 1885 eleven year old Joseph Kekuku found a loose steel bolt as he walked a railroad track. As he slid the bolt along the strings of his guitar, the unusual sound intrigued him. Over the next seven years, he created and then mastered the world famous Hawaiian steel guitar, sharing his discovery with others. By 1904 he had become so accomplished on the instrument that he played major theaters from coast to coast, then went to Europe to play for eight years before the royalty of different countries.

Kekuku became an early worldwide ambassador of Hawaiian music, and the distinctive sound of the steel guitar would become the sound of Waikiki via Hollywood films and radio broadcasts. Inevitably the soaring sound of steel found its way into blues, jazz, country music, and rock and roll, making a major contribution to American music. [21]

THE DANCING FLEA

In 1878 a tiny musical curiosity imported from the island of Madeira arrived to reshape Hawaiian music. When Portuguese contract laborers ambled off the ship playing the *braguinha*, a small four string instrument with metal strings, Hawaiians immediately took to it. The lively melodies coming from the instrument led Hawaiians to call it the *'ukulele*, or jumping flea. When fitted with strings of gut, the *'ukulele* became a featured instrument in the Merry Monarch's band. [20]

Duke Kahanamoku's *'ukulele*, at the Bishop Museum.

A pineapple shaped *'ukulele*.

INVENTORS AND INVENTIONS

In an era when Thomas Edison was capturing the concept of electric lighting and Alexander Graham Bell was inventing the telephone, Kalakaua had a fascination with advances in technology and agriculture. He made sketches of ideas for inventions — a bottle cap, a fish-shaped torpedo. He designed ships, imported an expert on coffee to help its cultivation in the islands, and had inventor Thomas Edison's new phonograph exhibited before the royal court.

Inevitably, the Merry Monarch's extravagance created some friction — $15,000 for his birthday party, $150,000 for his yacht, $10,000 for a gold crown plus an expensive coronation, $320,930 to build 'Iolani Palace. In 1886 the king invited Edison to electrify 'Iolani Palace, and while sugar planters saw it as excessive government spending, the palace was lighted on July 21, 1886. Later Edison's film crew would bring his new fangled Vitascope to film scenes in Waikiki. Edison's film clips from 1898 appear in the documentary film, *Waikiki, In the Wake of Dreams*.

Right: This telephone was installed either in 'Iolani Palace or Kalakaua's boathouse, Healani, at Honolulu Harbor.
Below left: 'Iolani Palace, shortly after its completion in 1882.
Below right: The Palace illuminated at night.

Long Branch Bath's famous slide.

Waikiki Villa, circa 1920.

Poster announcing Van Tassell's *"daring"* performance that would eventually lead to his death.

Above: Waikiki Globe Hotel

An early trolley in Waikiki.

The Park Beach Hotel.

The modern age brought attempts at manned balloon flights in Kapiʻolani Park, the first in 1889 by a man named Melville, whose hot air balloon failed to take him aloft. Later that year, a fellow named Van Tassell soared some 5,000 feet over Kapiʻolani Park, and parachuted safely down. When he tried the same thing two weeks later, he parachuted into Keʻehi Lagoon and drowned. [22]

The commercial possibilities of Waikiki now began to draw the attention of merchants and hoteliers. James Dodd established the Long Branch Baths, a crude cottage where bathers changed their clothes for a small charge, on the site of today's Moana Hotel. The Long Branch featured a 40-foot high slide that sent beachgoers shooting 100 feet out into the water. Others saw business possibilities in building bath houses along Waikiki's shores — the Ilaniwai Baths along Kuhio Beach, the Waikiki Villa, where the Sheraton Waikiki is today, the Saratoga Baths, near today's Outrigger Reef Hotel, and the Old Waikiki, presently the site of the Hilton Hawaiian Village. In 1888, the Park Beach Hotel arrived where the Elks Club stands today below Diamond Head. Five years later, there was a hotel at Sans Souci. [23]

In this era, getting to Kapiʻolani Park by trolley from the Honolulu Post Office cost ten cents. Carriage service from Honolulu cost $1.50. Casual service was available from downtown via the Tally Ho wagon/trolley from Jim Dodd's saloon at Fort and Hotel Streets along King to Waikiki through taro patches and banana groves, swampland, and duckponds.

PRINCESS PAUAHI

Waikiki still had its reputation as a place of healing or convalescence. In the summer of 1884, Princess Bernice Pauahi Bishop returned from San Francisco, where she had had an operation to remove a malignant tumor. She stayed at her home in Waikiki and, terminally ill, wrote her will, leaving her estate to establish Kamehameha Schools for the children of Hawai'i, a trust with an endowment now worth over five billion dollars.

Bernice Pauahi Bishop died in Waikiki on October 16, 1884. A little over a century later Kamehameha Schools, her legacy, would be educating thousands of native Hawaiian children.

In January of 1889 Robert Louis Stevenson arrived, stayed in Waikiki at Sans Souci, and shared some memorable times with Kalakaua.

"What is more dangerous than sea bathing is entertaining and being entertained by his majesty, who is a very fine, intelligent fellow, but, oh! what a crop for the drink. He carried it like a mountain with a sparrow on its shoulders. Five bottles of champagne in three hours and a half, and the sovereign quite presentable, although perceptibly more dignified at the end." [24]

His Majesty King Kalakaua and Robert Louis Stevenson share some quiet moments.

Whatever the difference between the private man and the public man, in 1889 Kalakaua was plagued by controversy. He now was rumored to have received $75,000 personally for handing out an opium license. Gossip suggested that the king hosted wild parties with liquor and girls dancing "the lascivious hula." While Stevenson brought his own properly Victorian mother as a guest to some of these affairs, the negative news commentaries and talk eroded the king's image, contributing to his loss of political power.

For some, Waikiki was suspect: people there always seemed to be having a good time, and for local puritans, that was a sure clue that something had to be wrong. Responding to a newspaper comment criticizing the hotel at Sans Souci as a "disorderly house," Stevenson wrote a letter to the editor saying that, to the contrary, the most uncivilized thing he had encountered at the hotel was the persistent interruption of a telephone "bleating like a deserted infant." [25]

Stevenson had become friends with Kalakaua, Lili'uokalani, Archibald Cleghorn, Likelike (Cleghorn's wife and Kalakaua's sister), and young Princess Ka'iulani, memorializing the grace of this extraordinary girl by writing her a poem.

As Waikiki's reputation grew, a series of darker incidents cast long shadows across the easy going life here.

In 1891, after David Kalakaua's induction into the Order of Masons in San Francisco, he became ill and died at age 54. With an Edison recording phonograph at his bedside during his final hours, he sent his last words to his subjects: "Tell them I tried." [26] Some 70,000 people thronged the streets of San Francisco outside his funeral at Trinity Church.

His sister Lili'uokalani accepted the throne, but in a mere two years, in 1893, the Hawaiian Kingdom was overthrown and replaced by a Provisional Government run by Americans living in Hawai'i. News of the overthrow and of Lili'uokalani's protests made headlines across America. Ironically, the Queen's own campaign to encourage links with the mainland and increase tourism was realized.

In the decade prior to her overthrow, visitors averaged 2,200 a year. At the turn of the century, Matson added dedicated passenger service, and soon visitors averaged 5,400 annually. [27]

The early part of the century also saw the Queen's hopes for a telegraph cable to the United States realized — one was brought ashore in Waikiki at Sans Souci in 1902.

THE BATTLE OF DIAMOND HEAD

Not everyone was willing to give up so easily on the kingdom. On the night of January 6, 1895 Royalists hoping to restore the monarchy smuggled in guns at Sans Souci, below Diamond Head. George Lycurgus, Prince Jonah Kuhio, Henry Bertlemann, and 150 Royalists gathered to revolt. But when word of their plans reached the sheriff, he sent the Republican militia to catch the rebels. After an exchange of shots, the battle shifted to the slopes of Diamond Head. Outnumbered and outgunned, the Royalists fled to Palolo and Manoa, and two days later surrendered.

Two Royalists died, and 200 supporters of the Queen were

Above: Princess Ka'iulani, holding hat.
Left: Prince Jonah Kuhio Kalanianaole.

arrested. Prince Jonah Kuhio and George Lycurgus went to prison, and the Queen was placed under house arrest for several months. Sans Souci became a victim as well, and went out of business as a hotel. Out of the frying pan, Greek-born Lycurgus ended up on the island of Hawai'i, where he jumped into the fire, taking over the Volcano House.

END OF AN ERA

At the turn of the century, major industrial powers were well on their way to gobbling up whatever foreign territories they could. The United States pursued its expansionist policy of "Manifest Destiny" by declaring war on Spain, seizing Guam, and invading the Philippines. Urged on by major sugar producers in the islands, President McKinley signed the Newlands Joint Resolution of Annexation of Hawai'i, making it a U.S. Territory. Hawaiians gathered 21,000 signatures on a petition protesting annexation, but Congress and President McKinley simply ignored them. In Waikiki kids still spoke Hawaiian, but under a 1900 law — ironically called the Organic Act — the Territory banned the language from classrooms and playgrounds, where youngsters were punished for using it.

As fighting in the Philippines extended into the 20th century, the tents of soldiers on their way to and from the war filled Kapi'olani Park for five years. With Diamond Head commanding access by sea to Honolulu, the U.S. military would soon establish Fort Ruger behind the promontory, and dredge coral to make a place for shore batteries at Fort DeRussy in Waikiki.

Two views of Army tents in Kapi'olani Park

A DAY AT THE RACES

Led by Alexander Young, the new Kapiʻolani Park Commission improved both the racetrack and waterways, added a new polo field, planted more trees, and created tennis courts and baseball fields. *Paradise of the Pacific* wrote, "In the park during the moonlit nights of each month the famous Hawaiian Band gives concerts which draw crowds of people in carriages, on horseback, and on bicycle; here also is the racetrack where each year the Hawaiian Jockey Club holds it meetings." [30]

While Hawaiians had gambled on sports at Waikiki in the days of Kamehameha the Great, horse races now provided a major attraction. [31] Lemon "Rusty" Holt remembered it this way.

"The race track . . . started Diamond Head side and went all the way down to . . . the zoo . . . those horses were really, really beautiful . . . the whole place was jam packed. Betting was open to whoever had gold and silver coins, *kala* . . . Everybody bet, even the chief of police was underneath the grandstand betting on the race . . . Anybody who had money bet, shook hands, and that was it . . . It was funny, I noticed big guys like the chief of detectives and the chief of police, they were on one side of the grandstand, and on the other side . . . were the supposedly small polloi, like plain officers and plain people . . . The majority of the people attending those horse races were families." [32]

KAʻIULANI

At Ainahau, Princess Kaʻiulani's peacocks became the inspiration for the name of her favorite flower, *pikake*. Off Waikiki, the young Kaʻiulani would be seen surfing on her big *olo* board, and at night she would take her evening swim — first placing a flower on one of the healing stones. [28]

The overthrow of the monarchy and annexation had left Kaʻiulani with little hope of ever achieving the throne. In the early hours of a February morning in 1899, her peacocks mysteriously began a wild and sustained wailing. The lovely young queen-to-be died at age 23. Although Queen Liliʻuokalani lived on, Princess Kaʻiulani's untimely death signaled the end of monarchy in Hawaiʻi.

A cutting from the huge banyan tree at Ainahau was used to start a sister banyan tree that today grows on the grounds of Kaʻiulani Elementary School. Beneath it lies a bronze plaque that was moved from Ainahau and reads:

Princess Kaʻiulani

"This Tablet Was Placed in Memory of Princess Kaʻiulani 1875-1899. The Daughter of a Double Race, Her Islands Here, in Southern Sun, Shall Mourn Their Kaʻiulani Gone, And I, in Her Dear Banyan Shade, Look Vainly for My Little Maid.' Written to Kaʻiulani by Robert Louis Stevenson, Who Often Sat Here with Her." [29]

On the corner of Kuhio and Kaʻiulani Avenues in Waikiki, a statue of the Princess graces a small park at the site of her family estate, Ainahau.

COALS FROM NEWCASTLE

The new century brought automobiles, trolleys, Hollywood movies, and more importantly, ships carrying more passengers. Matson now provided travelers with four passenger and freight steamers per month to the islands. The Hawaiian Glee Club toured U.S. cities, featuring the talents of 'ukulele players, putting Waikiki and the islands on the map for potential visitors.

The 1890's mule-drawn streetcar to Waikiki gave way to Honolulu Rapid Transit's electric ones in 1903. In order to attract more fares, HRT shareholders opened the Waikiki Aquarium on the beach below Diamond Head in 1904.

Paradise got another palace, this one for visitors, as the majestic Moana Hotel rose in 1901 under the guiding hand of W.C. Peacock. Waikiki had never seen anything like it. Its 75 rooms boasted modern conveniences — separate baths, electric lights, a roof garden, and amazingly, telephones.

At about 2 A.M. on the morning of August 11, 1910, the British barkentine *Helga* — on her way from Newcastle with a full cargo of coal for San Francisco — went aground off Waikiki. For years the beach-boys called the Moana "The only hotel ever to sink a ship." Although the captain ultimately denied it, the story was that he mistook the Moana's rooftop lights for those of the lighthouse at Honolulu Harbor.

Clockwise from top: The Moana under construction circa 1901; Kalakaua Avenue circa 1905; aerial view of the Moana clearly showing its famous pier, and the Moana bungalows circa 1913.

49

In many ways Waikiki reflected Kalakaua's vision of cultural renewal in a place free of cares. He left a valuable legacy in Waikiki where Hawaiians could enjoy the best of life — nature's beauty, water sports, festivals, band music, leisure, horse races, a spectacular park, and outsiders invited to join the fun. Today a fine statue of Kalakaua greets visitors from the small triangular park on the corner of Kalakaua and Kuhio Avenues, at the entrance of Waikiki, a fitting recognition for the Merry Monarch.

As if to reinforce that Hawai'i was an integral part of America's west, the country's best cowboys competed in Honolulu's first Wild West Show at Kapi'olani Park in 1905, to the delight of 3000 spectators. Hawai'i's *paniolo* realized they could compete with any cowpoke in the world, and three of them went to Wyoming to dominate the famous Frontier Days Rodeo at Cheyenne in 1908.

Right: The vaquero influence is evident in this photo of an early *paniolo* (cowboy).

Left: King David Kalakaua's statue welcomes visitors at the entrance of Waikiki.

Left: 1914. Henry Berger (standing), James Dole, Her Majesty Queen Liliʻuokalani and Governor Lucius Pinkham.
Inset: Berger proudly poses with his prized "Order of Kamehameha" medal, among others.

Under the baton of German-born Henry Berger, the Royal Hawaiian Band evolved into a superb musical ensemble, and a unique and popular feature of Waikiki. Good enough to export, in 1905 the band set sail for the mainland. Two Oregon papers commented:

"The dusky-skinned musicians made their first bow yesterday . . . applause was generous . . . enthusiastic crowds hung around the bandstand all the time the Hawaiians played and sang."

Oregon Daily Journal, Sept. 8, 1905

"Talk about versatility! The most remarkable Royal Hawaiian Band began an engagement at the Lewis & Clarke Exposition yesterday. People can hear a brass band any day — but they cannot hear music like this more than once in a lifetime."

Morning Oregonian, Sept. 18, 1905.

Hawaiʻi was inching into the modern world, but for those who loved the beach, Waikiki remained what Mark Twain captured when he wrote, "remote from the work-day world . . . forever smiling out on the sparkling sea . . . forever inviting you." [33]

CHAPTER **4**

COMING OF AGE

I heard the beachboys singing, sweet music filled the air.
Ethel Philipps in *Star Bulletin* "Our Own Poets" feature, 1932

With the prose of Stevenson and Twain, mainland tours by island musicians with their steel guitars and ukuleles, and the *Paradise of the Pacific* monthly touting her delights, Waikiki's idyllic image continued to permeate the nation's consciousness.

Missionary zeal and a western system of values had left both surfing and paddling as casualties. While preachers discouraged the sports as idle, beachboys nonetheless began to find it profitable to sell canoe rides and surfing lessons. A champion surfer and fine musician named Edward Kaleileihealani "Dudi" Miller of the Hui Nalu Surf Club pioneered surfing lessons for tourists. Surfing attracted visitors, and a beachboy culture began to emerge in Waikiki. A turn-of-the-century commentator wrote of surfing, "It was the Hawaiians of all the sons of the earth . . . who discovered its subtle power and the subtle power to control it." [1]

Writer Jack London was already famous when he reached Waikiki in 1908 on his sailboat *Snark*. He stayed in a tent at the Seaside Hotel, and later, afloat in the warm sun of Pearl Harbor, wrote his famous story "To Build A Fire," ironically about a man freezing to death in Alaska. London was captivated by Waikiki's majestic waves and the Hawaiians' ability to ride them, and he penned a piece called "The Royal Sport: Surfing at Waikiki" for a national magazine. He wrote:

"Why they are a mile long, these bull-mouthed monsters, and they weigh a thousand tons, and they charge in to shore faster than a man can run . . . I heard the crest of the wave hissing and churning, and then my board was lifted and flung forward . . . I could not see anything, for I was buried in the rushing white of the crest. But I did not mind. I was chiefly conscious of ecstatic bliss at having caught the wave." [2]

Original Outrigger Canoe Club.

Charmaine and Jack London, Alexander Hume Ford with friends, Outrigger Canoe Club, circa 1915.

He befriended surfer George Freeth, and with Alexander Hume Ford, formed The Outrigger Canoe Club. Starting with one grass hut to store canoes and another as a dressing room, the exclusive club boasted 1200 members by 1915. A rival canoe club, Hui Nalu, was soon formed primarily by native Hawaiian watermen.

Beachboys worked for tips, teaching visitors how to surf, giving outrigger canoe rides, acting as escorts, musicians, trusted companions and confidants. They would become as impressive a natural attraction as Diamond Head.

With seaweed (*limu*), all kinds of fish (*papio, ulua, ono, kumu*), squid and octopus fresh from the ocean, there was plenty to eat — and then there were Waikiki's moonlit nights under the sway of the palms. Beachboys gathered in front of the wall near the Moana Hotel to sing, talk story, fish and share good times with visitors. John D. Kaupiko, Dad Center, Dudie Miller, George Freeth, Pua Kealoha, Steamboat Bill, Tough Bill, the Hollinger boys and the Kahanamoku boys were a few of the originals who made Waikiki Waikiki. [3]

Surfers carved their redwood or pine boards out of solid planks. Designs returned to those of earlier Hawaiians, and boards were extended out to ten feet, akin to the ancient chiefs' *olo* boards. Big boards became a status symbol. Beachboys shellacked them with the juice of the *ti* plant, the old fashioned way. The boards eventually gave way to Tom Blake's design for a 16-foot hollow board, then a board with a fin, and with demand for boards on the rise, designers began to create the boards we see today all over the world. [4]

Soon there were surfing carnivals, contests where winners rode the waves standing on their heads or surfing in tandem.

Beachboy-musician Aunae Noa Kepoikai "Freckles" Lyons Sr. (standing) surfs off Waikiki.

Famed waterman Tom Blake in front of the Waikiki Villa, circa 1926.

Outrigger canoeing had resurfaced as well, and now surf breaks at Waikiki acquired names like Castles, Zero Breaks, Steamer Lanes, Cunha Surf, and Canoe Surf. [5] They had few material possessions, but beachboys of this era showed that the combination of Hawaiian culture and Waikiki made it possible to live the dream of a carefree life. Surveying the upsurge in visitors, Jack London wrote, "Some day Waikiki Beach is going to be the scene of one long hotel." His prophecy would come true in ways no one then dared dream.

BEAUTY VS. GRAVITY

After the Spanish-American War and the subsequent revolt in the Philippines, the U.S. military beefed up its presence in Hawai'i, and shipped their latest weapon to the islands — airplanes. One of the Kahanamoku girls had drawn the attention of a young Army pilot. To impress her, he flew his new biplane low across the *surf* line in front of the Moana Hotel. When the tail of the plane accidentally dipped into the water, he smashed into the pier. He was lucky to walk away from the first plane crash caused by a Waikiki bathing beauty. [6]

Surfboard polo game at
The Royal Hawaiian, circa 1930.

ENTER THE DUKE

The value of ocean sports in Waikiki had become all the clearer when the Queen Emma Estate leased a lagoon plus one and a half acres between the Moana's pier and what would later be The Royal Hawaiian Hotel: the sole purpose — sheltering surfboards and outrigger canoes from the elements.

By 1911, one of the Kahanamoku brothers, Duke, began to develop a reputation as a swimmer. He turned in a 100 yard freestyle time of 55.4 seconds, a full 4.6 seconds faster than the existing world record. Mainland amateur athletic officials scoffed at his times, but in 1912 he qualified for three Olympic events: the 100 and 200 meters, and the 800 meter relay. At the Stockholm games, he won the 100 meters despite being slow off the blocks, beating the Olympic record by three seconds. When the relay race approached, teammates couldn't find Duke, who was catching a nap behind the stands. A teammate found and woke him just in time for Duke to swim the anchor lap, yielding the team a silver medal in the 4 x 200 meter freestyle relay. [7]

From then on, Duke Kahanamoku was an international celebrity, introducing surfing to the east coast of the U.S., Australia, New Zealand, and California. During World War I he traveled across America raising war bond money. [8] Duke came to embody the image of the carefree bronzed waterman, the best Hawai'i had to offer, an example of how Waikiki with its surf, sand, and spirit of aloha, could shape a man.

Below: While the stately Moana dominates the shoreline (right), much of Waikiki was duckponds and rice paddies. Their products — ducks, duck eggs and rice — provided food for the Chinese population.

A DREAM OF SOMETHING BETTER.

Dreams don't always work out the way the dreamer imagines. With more buildings and visitors came difficult choices about Waikiki's future. In 1913 road work and construction along Waikiki cut off drainage from the agricultural wetlands, leading Chinese farm laborers to dig a trench that released a flood of stagnant water and duck pond muck onto the beach near the Moana Hotel. Tourists complained, and Governor Lucius Pinkham began serious planning for a way to drain the marshy backwaters and design Waikiki as a major resort.

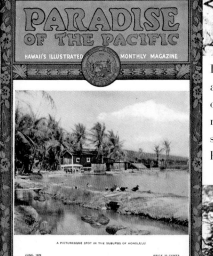

PARADISE OF THE PACIFIC
HAWAII'S ILLUSTRATED MONTHLY MAGAZINE

A PICTURESQUE SPOT IN THE SUBURBS OF HONOLULU.

JUNE, 1929.   PRICE 25 CENTS

Left: Duck ponds grace a *Paradise of the Pacific* cover, June 1929. Caption reads "A picturesque spot in the suburbs of Honolulu."

Mosquito Guards, circa 1913.

Although Waikiki had duckponds, 15 commercial fishponds, and many acres of rice paddies, it was clear that agriculture and tourism could never be comfortable bedfellows. Mosquitoes and polluted water were not only annoying; they posed serious health problems.

For those who saw past the rice paddies and duck ponds, the direction of Waikiki's future was becoming clear. Kapi'olani Park now had a zoo to accompany its popular Waikiki Aquarium. The Waikiki Tavern and Outrigger Canoe Club pavilion were built, and, on property formerly owned by royalty, a Scotsman named George MacFarlane added a group of cottages and called it the Seaside Hotel. Local and visiting socialites spent Sunday afternoons in the friendly surf there. Later, part of King David Kalakaua's lands off the beach were sold to develop the Royal Grove subdivision, with lots priced between $925 and $1500 each.

A duck farm in Waikiki, circa 1920.

THE KAMEHAMEHA PAGEANT & THE BIRTH OF THE MODERN BATHING SUIT

Tourism promoters held a carnival and parade in Waikiki in 1914, and set the stage for the more elaborate pageant of the following year, a full scale reenactment of Kamehameha's conquest of O'ahu, complete with warriors coming ashore in canoes (below.) Some of the pageant organizers feared displaying bare skin, and Hawaiians celebrating their own history wore long underwear for the occasion. Ironically, the history of beach clothing in Waikiki soon swung in the opposite direction, a direction no fashion designer of the era would have dared take.

PARADISE OF THE PACIFIC
June, 1913
THE WAIKIKI GIRL

When a helpful passerby returned the bathing gowns of several young ladies from the end of the Moana Pier to the hotel, the women had to come ashore with arms, legs, and shoulders unveiled. A wave of shock ran down the beach, but soon women decided they too would enjoy the freedom of movement and comfort, and many began wearing men's bathing attire as part of a sleeveless, bathing suit sans bloomers and stockings. Reverend Stephan Desha and other outraged protectors of public decency railed against the new fashion. The short-lived 1921 Desha Bathing Suit Act outlawed wearing bathing attire on Honolulu's streets, but it was too late. The women of Honolulu persisted, and the law was soon overturned. Men quietly rejoiced, for Waikiki had just given birth to the modern woman's bathing suit. For nearly twenty years the area near the Moana, Halekulani and Royal Hawaiian was called Flappers' Acres. [9]

An Advertising Dream Come True

Using a $100,000 appropriation from the legislature, the Waikiki Promotion Committee set up a pavilion at the 1915 International Exposition in San Francisco. On his *'ukulele*, Henry Kailimai played his composition, *On the Beach at Waikiki*, while hula dancers illustrated what awaited visitors in the islands. Kailimai's song became a major national hit, and with it went images of swaying hulas and Diamond Head. [10] In a marketing coup undreamed before or since, several million Exposition visitors heard the *'ukulele*, and suddenly it became a national fad, eventually selling by the hundreds of thousands along with sheet music and how-to-play-the-uke books. The humble Portuguese *braguinha* from Madeira had transformed into a symbol of Hawaiian culture, and now it had gone nationwide.

MUSIC, MUSIC, MUSIC

The sudden national success of Hawaiian music demonstrated how the fate of Waikiki remained tied to Hawaiian culture, for island music was an export that attracted visitors. New York's Tin Pan Alley generated songs on Hawaiian themes (*Yaka Hula Hicky Dula*), and Hawaiian sheet music sold from Bangor to Birmingham. Ukuleles were now manufactured as far away as Nazareth, Pennsylvania, by the fabled Martin Company. [11]

In half a dozen years, the humble instrument of beachboys became part of many band arrangements and vaudeville shows around the country. A decade later, Roy Smeck, one of the 'ukulele's most renowned non-Hawaiian artist of the era, had a 26 week engagement at New York's Radio City Music Hall, performing everything from *12th Street Rag* to *Stars and Stripes Forever*. [12] Smeck's showmanship and virtuosity inspired the sale of tens of thousands of ukes for the Harmony Company of Chicago.

The music of the islands gained national momentum. Charles E. King wrote hundreds of songs, including *Song of the Islands*, and he became known as the father of Hawaiian composers.

A young Hawaiian Yale alumnus named Sonny Cunha adapted the old *Moanalua Hula* into *Boola, Boola*, and it became Yale's school song. Returning home, Cunha added piano to ragtime arrangements, creating an upbeat, *hapa-haole* (part foreign/part local) sound that quickly gained popularity. Cunha's fame as a bandleader attracted Johnny Noble to his orchestra in 1918, and Noble brought a new jazz sensibility to Hawaiian music and orchestration. Modern Hawaiian music was born. [13]

Sheet music became major advertising for the islands, and the humble 'ukulele emerged as the 1920's symbol of good times — the snazzy college playboy with his raccoon coat, a flapper on his arm, and his 'ukulele in hand.

Meanwhile, an extraordinary steel guitarist named Sol Ho'opi'i, carried this special sound of the islands to Hollywood just as Hawaiiana became a national rage. There were even stories of Mary Pickford relying on Ho'opi'i's mournful steel guitar to help her weep on cue. [14]

THE CARRIAGE TRADE
GOES TO THE BEACH

In the first quarter of the century, wealthy industrialists from America's Gilded Age found their way to the islands, including Henry Ford and his friend Thomas Edison. When the Halekulani Hotel, the "House Befitting Heaven," was built in 1917, local musicians flocked to perform in the relaxed grace of the Hau Tree Lanai. As Hollywood discovered Waikiki, greeting visitors on Boat Day became a Honolulu tradition. Charlie Chaplin, the famous funny man of the era, couldn't resist the world's most famous beach, nor could countless other silent screen stars. To the delight of Honolulu residents, the Little Tramp spotted a popular dancing traffic cop downtown and spent an hour imitating him directing traffic on Bishop Street.

Buildings along the beach began to change as wealthy families began spending their leisure time at Waikiki. Beneath Diamond Head the Castle estate extended out over the shallows on a site that now houses both the Outrigger Canoe club and Elks Club. The W.G. Irwin home later became the site of the War Memorial Natatorium.

Despite World War I, women getting the vote, Prohibition, a devastating international flu epidemic, and more revealing female attire on the beach, Waikiki had somehow remained only slightly altered. Thousands of people continued to ride

Charlie Chaplin during one of his many Hawai'i trips, here in 1917, amid young Hawaiian admirers.

Boat Day! Hundreds of Honoluluans gather to welcome the arrival of a steamer.

But Kathleen Hall, CEO of The Stress Institute, says "taking time for vacation and leisure is not a luxury. It is a necessity. The chronic stress of work can lead to emotional and physical illness."

How do you leave work behind? Hall suggests:

1. Encourage your spouse, children and co-workers to remind you to "detach and disconnect".

2. If you can't leave behind your work responsibilities, check e-mail or call the office only at scheduled times, then resume your vacation.

3. Limit your use of BlackBerry devices and laptops.

4. Tell clients you're away, and designate another contact person.

the trolley down Kalakaua Avenue lined with shower trees and palms — to the beach or to lovely Kapiʻolani Park, with its beautiful reflecting pools and lily ponds, horse races, and polo games on Saturday afternoons.

WAIKIKI THE NEIGHBORHOOD

Waikiki in the teens and early twenties still had fish ponds, rice paddies, taro and watercress patches, banana groves, duck ponds, and plenty of mosquitoes! And there was open space. On Kalia and Lemon Roads, there were distinctly Hawaiian neighborhoods with family homes and a few mom-and-pop stores. [18]

The Center for Oral History, University of Hawaiʻi's *Waikiki: 1900-1985* provides us valuable glimpses of early 20th century life here. Earl Vida offered this picture of a sleepy Waikiki:

"Now when we went to school, we'd . . . go across the duck ponds . . . because there no roads in those days. The *poi* factory was near the Kalauokalani's . . . where the old stream used to run . . . All of us that lived on the beach, our food right from the ocean. Of course we raised pigs and stuff like that. I had a little piggery there", and mother would kalua a pig. Planted everything in the ground, potatoes, tomatoes, everything right there. It's all semi-sand . . . You see, was all ocean at one time." [19]

During hard times, Hawaiians like Rebecca Kapule did what they had always done. "We women folks used to go out (to) catch seaweed and one of the women would be home cooking lunch. So we all come back with whatever we catch — and sit under the hau tree and we start cleaning seaweed. At the meantime, everybody's joking or revealing old stories." [20]

DUKE

Duke Kahanamoku was now to swimming and surfing what Babe Ruth was becoming to baseball. On a glassy morning at Waikiki in 1917, a set of huge waves suddenly appeared while Duke and Dad Center surfed far offshore near Diamond Head. Dad took the first wave, then Duke rode for half a mile, nearly all the way to The Royal Hawaiian Hotel: "It looked as though it would break on us and we started paddling out, then stopped and decided to chance it. It took just one stroke to catch it; I had to slide hard to get out of the break. I went so fast the chop of the wave struck the bottom of my board like the patter of a machine gun. I figured I was going about thirty miles an hour." [15]

In the 1920 Olympics, Duke Kahanamoku earned another gold medal for a world record time in the 100 yard sprint, adding another medal in the 4 x 200 meter relay. At age 34, he was edged out by Johnny Weissmuller in the 1924 games, taking the silver instead. Over his career Duke accumulated a total of six Olympic medals and became a member of the Olympic Hall of Fame. He also became the unofficial ambassador for the islands, handling victory, defeat, and acclaim with a grace that made him legendary. [16] In 1925, off Corona Del Mar, California, Duke paddled out repeatedly into giant surf that had swamped a fishing boat and saved eight people from drowning. News of his heroism added to his legend. [17]

With Duke as its centerpiece, Waikiki attracted surfers from California, who made the pilgrimage by steamship to experience for themselves the famous surf of Waikiki Beach.

Duke went on to be the Sheriff of Honolulu, reelected a dozen times, the man everyone asked to meet, from Charlie Chaplin and Amelia Earhart, to FDR and John Kennedy.

on a piece of paper, seal it, maybe hide it in his shoes — and then he'd deliver it to the man. They would all meet up in a certain place, like in the rice fields." [23]

Lemon "Rusty" Holt remembered Waikiki as home, a place where people came and became family, Hawaiian style. Their generosity meant that their house was always full.

"Another thing about Waikiki, my family all had friends . . . Whoever came, never went home. There was a Louis Pomeroy. When he was six years old, he came down to play with me, and he never went home. My mother raised him until he was 24 years old. He stayed. Whoever came, friends of the family, young guys — they stayed. There was Bill Mossman, Leslie Lemon, Dudie Miller, Fadden McKinney — they all came . . . they never went home." [24]

Esther Jackson Bader remembered:

"Everybody was trying to help each other out, you know . . . the women, their husbands, in most cases, were working at hotels. They were either cooks, or they were bartenders . . . Every time you look at Mama-san she's ironing, or she's outside hanging clothes, and you know it's not theirs. -— they're not ashamed of doing it. That was their way of making extra money." [21]

For Fred Paoa, nature provided much as it had for others in centuries past. "I used to get up at 5:30 in the morning. And I used to go to De Russy. There was a little pier that went out. Catch two or three papios. Come home, cook it for breakfast. Then go to work. What the hell's better than that? You tell me." [22]

As Joe Akana recalled, there were those who took their chances on dreams. "It was like the — numbers game. You see, the people who bet, they bet on dreams. Most of the people in Waikiki, the Hawaiians, if they dreamed of something at night, they waited for the runner. — And they tell the number — the *hua* —. They told him what they dreamed of — Then the runner would write down

ENGINEERING A DREAM

Governor Lucius Pinkham

Who among us can ever tell where a dream will lead? Since his days as health commissioner just after the turn of the century, Lucius Pinkham had dreamed of what he called the Waikiki Canal. He envisioned a veritable Venice of the Pacific, with a canal wide enough for yachts and racing boats. The huge civil engineering feat that Pinkham's dream set in motion would, over the years, reshape the economics and politics of Hawai'i, and through them, the lives of her people. Pinkham intended to make Waikiki's water quality acceptable, improve public health conditions, and transform Waikiki into a small, upscale beach community and resort. Elected Territorial Governor in 1913, he had the legislature appropriate $100,000 for dredging and a canal in 1918, and work began in the early 1920's.

Designs called for the canal to be 150 feet wide with a 75 foot boulevard on either side. The legislature purchased 340 acres at $83 to $400 an acre, and Walter Dillingham's Hawaiian Dredging Construction put in the winning bid of $22,560. [25]

Waikiki's substructure was a mix of ancient lava flows and old coral reefs. These carried the underground springs for which Waikiki had been named, and the springs fed the rich agricultural plots that checkered the area. From 1921 on, dredging for the new canal moved some 2.4 million cubic yards of coral, mud and sand, which Dillingham was delighted to sell to individuals, who were required by law to fill in their land. At 59 cents a cubic yard, the company grossed almost a million and a half dollars. Property values of the suddenly solid land escalated wildly, and many people — especially Hawaiians — lost their lands when they were unable to afford the new, higher property taxes. [26]

The completed canal stretched just under two miles, drained 16.3 square miles of land, and captured silt from three streams running

Above and right: Dredging the Ala Wai Canal. Below: The Canal exits to the sea at what is now the site of the Ala Wai Yacht Harbor.

into it. Plans called for it to be dredged every dozen years, and to have an exit on either end of Waikiki, but, as Earl Vida recalled, his father saved Waikiki's waters with some Hawaiian common sense. "They wanted to put the opening of the canal down towards Kapahulu Avenue. And Dad says, 'You foolish if you did that' On account of the sediment and all that comes off the mountains, and he said, 'You'd ruin the ocean down here at Waikiki at Kuhio Park' That's where the outfall was. 'It'll pollute all that water.' By God, they listened to him. And so they blocked it off at the Library near the fire station there. So when dad and them built the canal, they eliminated all that." [27]

Where natural waterways once converged and ran to the sea, there was now Kapahulu Avenue. Streams at each end had left part of Waikiki an island, but now the area was a peninsula separated from the rest of Honolulu by the canal.

In 1922 the Aloha Amusement Park opened on landfill near Ft. DeRussy. Between 1924 to 1929, a building boom started in Waikiki — prices shot up, even quadrupled, as shops and restaurants drew increasing crowds to the newly-created lands stretching to the beach.

Waikiki had come to mean beachboys, surfing, hula dancers, coconut trees, days of laughter and song at the beach, and moonlit nights of romance. But now, under the gaze of Diamond Head, much of it appeared as a baking plateau of gleaming crushed coral and sand in need of tropic foliage. Even the Garden of Eden had required a little work, and everyone recognized that here Paradise was a work in progress. Creating substantially more land and far less stagnant water, the canal's engineers at first lacked funds to complete any opening to the sea. Eventually, one was dug, and the canal was completed in 1928. Paradise had lost the stinking, flooding duck ponds and persistent mosquitoes. Land values skyrocketed from $500 to $25,000 a lot.

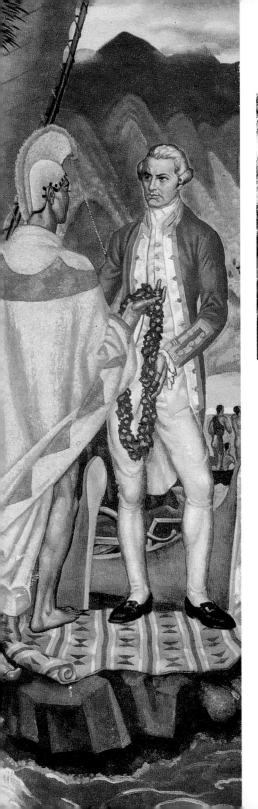

ADVERTISING PARADISE

Armed with $25,000 from the newly-formed Hawai'i Tourist Bureau, a young copywriter by the name of George Armitage set out to entice a steady flow of visitors to Waikiki, by advertising what he called, "the witchery of Native life, the spell of her natural wonders, the charm of her scenery and climate."

Once the government completed Honolulu's first high rise, Aloha Tower, in 1926, Matson Navigation Company envisioned full boats and full luxury hotels. The first generation of screen stars and directors joined wealthy vacationers from around the world for a dreamy glimpse of the moon rising over Diamond Head. With Hawai'i's advertisers now spending between $80,000 and $120,000 a year, visitor numbers grew 15% to 20% a year. 15,000 visitors a year in the 1920's meant that tourism now provided two percent of Hawai'i's economy. [28]

Above: Aloha Tower served as a lighthouse, the harbor traffic control office, and a welcoming landmark to visitors. At 163 feet, she was the tallest building in the Islands until the 1950s.

Left: In this art deco Matson menu cover by Eugene Savage, Kalaniopu'u offers Captain James Cook a lei of welcome at Kealakekua Bay.

Right: Covers from *Paradise of the Pacific* and a Hawai'i Tourist Bureau ad promoting Hawai'i's legendary sense of hospitality and Aloha spirit.

The Royal Hawaiian's *Persian Dining Room*, filled with guests during Opening Night gala in February, 1927.

THE ROYAL

With traffic rising on Matson's liners, the cottages of the Seaside Hotel gave way to the world renowned Royal Hawaiian. The building required 35,000 barrels of cement and 9,000 gallons of paint, and when it began to sink into the sand during construction, noted naval architect Admiral Frank Harris was called in to save it with reinforcing structures. Like its neighbor the Moana, The Royal Hawaiian had water from its own well. With its bellmen adorned in Chinese costumes, and tea served by young Japanese women in traditional *kimono*, the graceful Pink Palace opened in 1927. [29] Waikiki now boasted a $5 million, 400 room, four star hotel catering to everyone from the Duponts and Rockefellers to film stars Mary Pickford and Douglas Fairbanks. The Royal was in a class by itself. Its gala opening was described as the biggest event in Waikiki since the Oahu invasion of Kamehameha I. Rooms cost $14 a night. [30]

When an eccentric Waikiki resident took a room at the Royal, he insisted on driving his electric car through its wide halls. Legend holds that a kama'aina dowager offered to buy the hotel so she could tear it down and recapture the feeling of old Waikiki. But there would be no turning back.

THE DOLE CUP AIR RACE

The early history of aviation to the Islands was not encouraging. Piloting a rickety, sputtering aircraft over 2400 miles, then finding a tiny speck in the ocean, was a decidedly difficult task.

The Navy tried first in 1925. In a hurried effort to establish naval aviation as viable, they prepared four seaplanes for the long trek. Only two actually took off, and soon, just one — Commander John Rodgers PN-9 "Dreadnought"— was still airborne.

The Navy stationed ten ships across the Pacific along the intended route. These served both as a safety net and as "gas stations" for the planes to land and refuel. Rodgers, however, was determined to fly non-stop. Bad idea. Four hundred and fifty miles from the islands, his craft ran out of fuel and glided to a perfect ocean landing. When his radioman cranked the instrument to life to report their position, the crew soon realized that they could receive, but not send messages. They heard searchers frantically looking for them ... hundreds of miles away, headed in the other direction.

Running out of food and water, they converted their craft into a crude square-rigger, by stripping some of the canvas skin off the plane, then jerry-rigging sails between the upper and lower wing. By ripping up the floorboards and lashing them to the fuselage, they were able to create a rudder of sorts. Then — long after hope had given out — they sailed the plane to Kaua'i!

In 1927 a pair of Army fliers successfully landed on O'ahu, and just weeks later, two civilians — Ernest Smith and Emory Bronte — completed what is still the only non-stop flight between the mainland and Moloka'i, when they landed, unhurt, in a kiawe tree!

Enter Pineapple King James Dole. In the spirit of the times, he offered $35,000 in cash prizes to the first and second place winners of the first, and only, Transpacific Air Derby. Eight planes poised to take off in Oakland. Two crashed on the runway, two turned back, two were lost at sea. Only two of the eight contenders actually reached the islands. The winner, with a time of 27 hours, 16 minutes, was the *Woolaroc*. In second (and last) place was the *Aloha* whose crew had found the islands by dead reckoning. Some 30,000 residents cheered the arrival of the daring fliers in the early morning of August 17, 1927.

These dangerous early experiments did prove that the islands were accessible by air. Many of those to follow would land at John Rodgers Field, now called Honolulu International Airport.

Landing of the *Aloha* on O'ahu, August 17th, 1927.

This extraordinary photo shows James D. Dole (center), president of the Hawaiian Pineapple Company, presenting the $25,000 check to Arthur C. Goebel and Lieutenant Davis, (on his right), and the $10,000 check to Martin Jensen and Paul Schluter (on his left), winners of the "California-to-Hawai'i Hop" Race. The awards were made at the Royal Hawaiian Hotel, Waikiki, Honolulu, on August 19th, 1927.

The *Aloha* and the *Woolaroc* side by side on O'ahu airfield.

WWI MEMORIAL NATATORIUM

The Matson Navigation Company had just built The Royal Hawaiian and purchased the Moana, Waikiki's two luxury hotels. Matson's beautiful new liner *Malolo* could bring 650 guests at a speed of 22 knots. Her luxurious amenities included phones in each room, a swimming pool, two gymnasiums, theaters, elevators serving five decks, and a soda fountain.

It was 1928. Gumps opened as the first major retailer in Waikiki, Herbert Hoover was President, and the stock market boomed. Outrigger canoe races in Waikiki drew hundreds of spectators, and below Diamond Head the ultimate water sportsman, Duke Kahanamoku, dedicated the new World War I Memorial Natatorium with its salt water swimming pool. After Duke's baptism of the salt-water pool with a swim, Johnny Weissmuller and Buster Crabbe set records.

PROHIBITION DAYS

Ka'ahumanu had tried unsuccessfully to enforce temperance a century earlier. Now, Hawai'i embraced Prohibition as the law of the land. Duke's younger brother Louis soon found himself working as a prohibition agent.

"He said, "You going be deputy U.S. Marshall."

I said. "What?"

"Yeah, you going be."

"Was a lot of fun, Prohibition. Geez, at one time I took this guy right across of The Royal Hawaiian. I made the pinch. The guy had about ten cases of gin . . . But you can't touch that liquor . . . had lot of guys on the beach that drank. So I would give them, you know. Had lot of the Hawaiians, old Japanese guys . . . They lived down our way, but they all go down where I tell them . . .

The Natatorium in 1928. The diving platforms (in foreground) had four height levels.

And I come down with my truck. So we're going to break all these bottles. There were a lot of . . . big concrete boulders. So we aim for these things and miss purposely. Then the bottle will land in the water . . . When we come back in the afternoon after work, all these old guys were sitting out there, drunk like hell." [34]

"ISLE O' DREAMS", HAWAII

4A-H797

MESSAGES TO AMERICA

Radio made it to the Pacific. Ray Kinney, a fine singer with Johnny Noble's band, performed on the first Waikiki broadcast of a national radio show sponsored by Matson Navigation. Music of the islands wafted across America.

With the age of advertising, familiar visual themes — hula dancers, palm trees, bronzed surfers, and Diamond Head — resonated Waikiki's charms. Hawai'i was spending some $149,000 a year to entice 22,000 visitors a year, just a few more than had arrived at the peak of the old whaling days. [35] Unlike those of a century earlier, visitors of this era showed little inclination to riot or destroy property. Waikiki was delighted to find itself living Lucius Pinkham's dream as a visitor resort for the carriage trade, but such dreams have a way of dissolving in the harsh light of morning.

When Wall Street's market collapsed in 1929, the ensuing worldwide depression sent visitor traffic plummeting. [36] Paradise was looking at hard times.

THE MASSIE CASE

National news coverage of the controversial 1931 Massie Rape/Murder Case added to the damage caused by the Depression. In this ugly chapter of Waikiki's history, a young Navy wife wrongly accused five young local men of kidnapping and raping her in Waikiki, near Fort DeRussy. Conflicting evidence left the prosecution's case in tatters, but after the young men were released, one of them was kidnapped and murdered by Navy Lt. Thomas Massie, husband of the woman who had claimed the rape. During the ensuing murder trial of Massie and his mother-in-law, the presence of famous defense attorney Clarence Darrow and stories of racial tensions in Hawai'i created sensational news across the country. Massie admitted the killing. In a gesture that confirmed the worst fears of islanders about Eurocentric attitudes, Massie and his mother-in-law sipped champagne with Hawai'i's Governor as he commuted their sentences an hour after their convictions. [37]

CHAPTER 5

The Golden Era

After all is said and done, more is said than done.
Anonymous

Long time Kodak honcho in Hawai'i, Fritz Herman, responded to visitors' letters that their photos of Hawaiian dancers at nighttime luaus never turned out, by gathering some local performers and creating the daytime Kodak Hula Show. Here, tourists dance with Hilo Hattie.

A school teacher by trade, Claire Haile became Hilo Hattie, gathering national attention in the movie *Ma & Pa Kettle At Waikiki*, where she upstaged everyone in the film including Ma and Pa themselves! She often performed in Waikiki with the Kodak Hula Show.

In the mid-1930's, the shadow of the Depression began to lighten a little in Waikiki. By 1934 the Royal Hawaiian Glee Club entertained crowds in Kapi'olani Park. When FDR visited, Duke Kahanamoku took the President's son surfing. The Kodak Hula Show began next to the Waikiki Natatorium in 1937. One of the more remarkable success stories in radio history began when Webley Edwards took the reins of *Hawai'i Calls*, broadcast with a live audience of two thousand residents and visitors at the Banyan Court at the Moana Hotel, to millions of listeners across America. The Hawaiian musical program's popularity carried the image of Waikiki across the nation every Saturday night. With the sounds of real surf lapping at the shore between songs, Waikiki became a place the entire country listened to, dreamed of, even sang along with. As legendary steel guitarist Jerry Byrd puts it, "*Hawai'i Calls* did more for Hawaiian music than anything ever could . . . it painted such a great picture of Hawai'i. It doesn't seem like much here, but it does to someone in a snow bank in South Dakota." [1] Over the next forty years, *Hawai'i Calls* became the longest continuously broadcast radio program in America, going out over 600 stations until it closed down in the early 1970's.

Jerry Byrd, world famous steel guitarist as he appears in the documentary film, *Waikiki, In the Wake of Dreams.*

Webley Edwards created *Hawai'i Calls*, a radio show beamed round the world. The tireless Edwards was also a radio station manager, the CBS Pacific war correspondent, and a State Representative. Edwards' entire collection of *Hawai'i Calls* radio shows has been preserved by the McDiarmid family.

In this era of elaborately gilded movie theaters such as Graumann's Chinese on Hollywood Boulevard in L.A., Waikiki matched Hollywood's style. On August 20, 1936, architect C.W. Dickey's Waikiki Theater premiered its first film, *Against All Odds*, as a fountain played at the entrance and filmgoers admired signatures of Hollywood celebrities. Inside, paradise had reinvented itself. Night blooming cereus, papaya, *lauhala*, banana, hibiscus, *ti*, ferns, and other tropic foliage adorned the walls. Overhead was a replica of the night sky, and arched over the screen, which was framed by two real coconut palms, shone a painted rainbow. In the movies of Hawai'i in the 1920's and 1930's, Waikiki had gone to Hollywood in a big way. Now Hollywood had a place of its own in the heart of Waikiki.

Hollywood Goes Hawaiian

Meanwhile, in a Hollywood night club, a young bandleader and trumpeter from Nebraska was making a big impression on the Royal Hawaiian's manager, accepting an invitation to become the hotel's bandleader. Harry Owens began arranging classic Hawaiian songs, orchestrating a sound that would become internationally recognized as the modern sound of Waikiki. Owens wrote *Sweet Leilani* for his baby daughter. Bing Crosby recorded the song which became a major national hit, winning the 1937 Academy Award for Best Song, in the film *Waikiki Wedding*.

By now Hollywood had developed a long term love affair with the islands and particularly Waikiki, but the studios largely misunderstood the richness of Hawaiian culture. In a succession of films, carefree, unsophisticated Hawaiians seemed compelled to grin, dance the hula spontaneously, enjoy staged semi-authentic luaus, perform quasi-Hawaiian songs, and stir the fire goddess Pele into volcanic eruption.

Clara Bow, the "It" girl, started the trend in 1927 with *Hula*. *Bird of Paradise* followed in 1932 starring Joel McCrae and Dolores Del Rio, who danced topless with an abundant lei to cover her

Top: Waikiki Theatre.
Right: Royal Hawaiian Hotel bandleader Harry Owens

Below:
From the 1932 RKO film *Bird of Paradise* Dolores Del Rio performing her famous topless hula.

75

daring décolleté. *Waikiki Wedding* in 1937 starred Bing Crosby. Martha Raye. and Anthony Quinn. While the film offered a threadbare romantic plot. it gave crooner Crosby his first million seller. and left people all over the country whistling *Sweet Leilani*. In the film Crosby also sang a song called *Blue Hawai'i*, which Elvis would sing twenty-five years later in a movie of the same name.

Whatever the characters, plot, or quality of the film. the setting of the islands was a co-star. and the culture was exotic. Moviegoers from Kansas to Katmandu now had images of paradise dancing in their dreams.

Left: Bing Crosby on the *Waikiki Wedding* movie set.
Below: Beachboy Chick Daniels entertains the stars of the movie *Bird of Paradise*. Joel McCrae and Dolores Del Rio.

Hawai'i's Poet Laureate Don Blanding captured the mystique of the islands in widely-quoted verse. Blanding created May 1 as a Lei Day celebration, and lent his talents to the mythology of Waikiki:

"Oh, the southern Cross hangs over my door,
And the moon flings silver on the floor,
While the surf makes thunder along the beach,
And the rainbow's end is within my reach." [2]

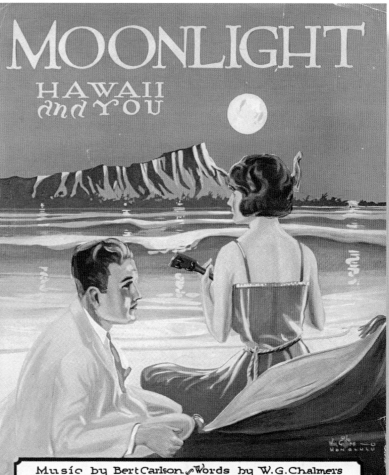

MOONLIGHT
HAWAII and YOU

Music by Bert Carlson Words by W. G. Chalmers
PUBLISHED BY THE
ALOHA PUBLISHING CO. HONOLULU T.H.

From sheet music to movies, romance has always been an essential ingredient in the magic of Waikiki. A still from *Blue Hawai'i* starring Elvis Presley and Joan Blackman (left) and the sheet music cover. *Moonlight Hawai'i and You.*

77

As always, beachboys' parties never lacked spirit. Almost every beachboy was an accomplished musician or singer.

Young Mickey Rooney with Panama Dave

BEACHBOY DAYS

For a flat fee of $750 a month, the Outrigger Canoe Club supplied services for guests of The Royal Hawaiian and Moana — food, a clubhouse, lockers, volleyball courts, a pavilion for dancing, and some legendary beachboys who seemed to know everyone. Fred Paoa, who grew up in Waikiki, recalled how a young man got into the business of being a beachboy.

"I think I was out there on the beach there as a beachboy, fifteen, sixteen . . . my cousins, Bill Kahanamoku, Sam, Duke, and David . . . they went out on the canoes, take the tourists out . . . I got to get on the canoes with them as second captain. We'd charge the tourists for going out, a dollar a head . . . And then we took surfboard lessons. I think we charged two dollars or two and a half an hour. That's how we made our money during the summertime."

"We caught fish. And we cooked 'em right under the *hau* tree . . . right next to the Moana Hotel. Made a fire. Put it on the charcoals . . . Everybody get poi, sit around. If the tourists want to join us, they'd come in and help themselves. No spoons (laughter) they liked it like that . . . Something different . . .

They'd bring their cars down from the mainland. These big cars — limousines. and have the fellow drive it. And all these Hawaiians sit there with bare feet and everything . . .

I used to take tourists slumming — Chinatown, all those places. Not for a fee, but I just did it to show them around. At night, you know . . . Go to the bars, the nightclubs . . . the Tin Can alley, Corkscrew Lane. And Hole-in-the-Wall . . . They enjoyed it."[3]

Joe Akana described life as a beachboy: "The Maharajah of Indore . . . came with his party of seventeen — when the Maharajah went, I went with them. Even his secretary and aide

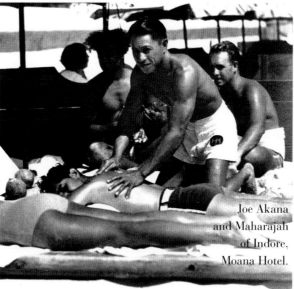

Joe Akana and Maharajah of Indore, Moana Hotel.

de camp were not allowed to ride in the same elevator. He was an Oxford graduate. His annual pay was his weight in gold . . . about $70 million dollars a year."[4]

Legendary 60's surf champion Fred Hemmings said of this era's beachboys: "The great appeal of these fun-loving guys was that they didn't care who you were or how much money you had . . . They wrote the book on fun."[5]

Visitors sincerely appreciated the kindness and aloha beachboys showered on them, and thousand dollar tips were not unheard of. Millionaire retailer Alfred Bloomingdale gave beachboy Panama Dave Baptiste a new Buick, a small acknowledgment of the good times they'd had playing gin rummy over the many years.

Although it hadn't been that long since Amelia Earhart made the first solo flight across the Pacific in 1935, airplanes had improved rapidly. Pan American's Clippers inaugurated passenger flights to Honolulu in 1936 with a flight time from San Francisco of 19 hours. Fares dropped from $712 round trip to $556, and before long

Continued on p.82

Pan Am clipper flying over Diamond Head, with the War Natatorium just below the plane and the Castle Estate on the far right.

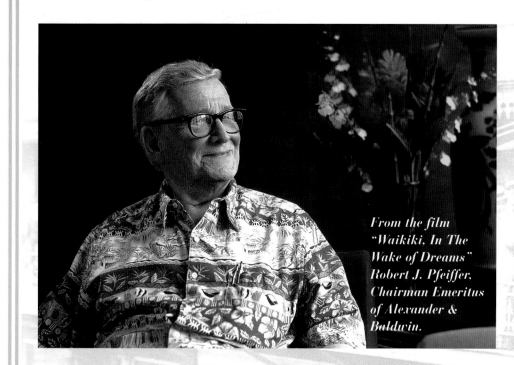

From the film "Waikiki, In The Wake of Dreams" Robert J. Pfeiffer, Chairman Emeritus of Alexander & Baldwin.

BOAT DAYS

The ritual of Boat Day arrivals and departures held lots of color. According to Robert J. Pfeiffer, Alexander & Baldwin Chairman Emeritus, "Practically everyone went down to the pier when a Matson ship came in. The *Lurline* and the *Matsonia* would come in. When they got off Waikiki, they would turn the bow into the beach by The Royal Hawaiian and blow three long blasts. Tugs would take reporters and people who bought a ticket to go out off shore to greet people and give them leis. And journalists would go out and interview big shots. It was very festive because you had outrigger canoes around and people coming aboard with leis. They'd proceed to the harbor. The Royal Hawaiian Band were there . . .

If you watched the women on the pier, the spectators, even if they didn't know anyone on the boat, as soon as the band played "Aloha Oe," they'd all start crying . . . [coin divers] were mostly Hawaiian boys, some haoles and Japanese. They would . . . congregate by the passenger ship before it was ready to sail, and people would throw coins over the side. Now a coin doesn't go straight down, it slants back and forth, so that if you're a good swimmer, you could catch the coin long before it hits bottom . . . The diving boys would get the coin, come back to the surface with big smiles, show the coin to whoever threw it, and then put it in their mouth. That's where they kept coins until they were through and got back on shore . . . They weren't too happy with a penny, but you know for twenty-five cents you could get a full lunch at the Eagle Cafe on Bethel Street . . . None of us ever dreamed that tourism would go the way it has." [7]

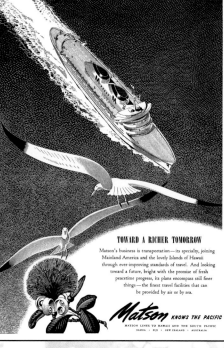

TOWARD A RICHER TOMORROW

Matson's business is transportation—its specialty, joining Mainland America and the lovely Islands of Hawaii through ever-improving standards of travel. And looking toward a future, bright with the promise of fresh peacetime progress, its plans encompass still finer things—the finest travel facilities that can be provided by air or by sea.

Matson KNOWS THE PACIFIC

MATSON LINES TO HAWAII AND THE SOUTH PACIFIC
SAMOA · FIJI · NEW ZEALAND · AUSTRALIA

Streamers cascade as the *Sierra* pulls away from the pier in 1912.

Aloha to the Lurline...and You

Steaming westward from California, you've gloried in the lazy days and lovely nights of your voyage . . . then your pulse quickens for this moment—landfall at sunrise. For islanders, it's home, the most beautiful home in the world . . . for visitors, the first view of these fairy-like Islands, rising rose-tinted in the tropic sea . . . and in a few moments, the flower-filled "Aloha" that Hawaii bestows on her beloved LURLINE.

There are many such memories on a Lurline cruise . . . and leaving Hawaii, staring a mainland vacation or on your way home again, you'll be with friends, sharing days of enchantment on the southern seas. With them you'll enjoy your air-conditioned stateroom; the luxurious cuisine and service; the movies, dancing, deck games, parties . . . all included in a Lurline round-trip fare.

Round Trip Fares as low as $260 plus tax

Matson Lines

See your Travel Agent or any Matson Lines office; Honolulu—Pier 11 • 2347 Kalakaua Ave. Phone 5-0945

THE LURLINE SAILS FROM HONOLULU EVERY TWELVE DAYS

Continued from p. 79

improved planes cut the time by two hours. Clippers landed at Pearl Harbor and used the seaplane ramps at Ford Island. Visitors who flew were still only a *manini* (tiny) one percent of all arrivals in Hawai'i. [6] But air travel to the islands was just beginning.

In the late 1930's visitors began to return in force, and Boat Days were in full swing. Celebrities arrived by the bushel: the Prince of Wales, Babe Ruth, Shirley Temple, Bing Crosby, Carole Lombard, George Burns and Gracie Allen, Groucho Marx, Eddie Cantor, Jimmy Durante, maharajahs, business barons, and just plain millionaires. And now they dressed a little differently when they came, for someone — probably a young Yale-educated Honolulu haberdasher named Ellery Chun — had created a loose, informal garment to match the island way of life — the aloha shirt.

Legendary musician, composer, and arranger Benny Kalama.

When he heard that Don McDiarmid, the Royal Hawaiian bandleader, was looking for a new singer, a young man named Alfred AhFat skipped school to audition. Musical legend Benny Kalama was present on that day when McDiarmid signed him. AhFat later changed his name to Apaka (many entertainers with Chinese surnames took Hawaiian family names because of immigration laws), and Waikiki gained a singer who would acquire lasting international fame. [8]

By now the beachboy subculture was a major influence in Waikiki, and beachboys gave one another names more colorful than those of Damon Runyon's New York gamblers and mobsters. Consider the roll call: Turkey, Chick, Panama Dave, Scooter Boy, Blue (and his surfing dog Night Hawk), Ox, Steamboat, Tugboat, Rowboat, Tough Bill, Dukie, and Colgate were just a few. And joining them on Waikiki beach John D. Kaupiko, Sr., Pua Kealoha and the Kahanamoku brothers.

Beachboys taught people to swim and surf, gave massages, babysat their kids, played music, took people on tours, and got to know folks so well that often they were invited to return with them to the mainland. They met the ships and scouted for "comebackers," returning visitors. Beachboys were good time guys with a relaxed dignity and visitors respected and loved them. Waikiki now blended island culture with mainstream American culture, as beachboys showed visitors the meaning of Hawaiian hospitality, the joy of living, and aloha. Laughter was never very far away.

Alfred Apaka performing at the Hilton Hawaiian Village. Behind him (left) is Benny Kalama.

U.S. Senator Daniel K. Inouye, as he appears in the film *Waikiki~In the Wake of Dreams.*

Little big star Shirley Temple receives the honorary title of Waikiki Beach Patrol Captain from Sally Hale and Pua Kealoha (standing), 1935.

BEACHBOY DAYS: U.S. SENATOR DANIEL K. INOUYE.

Dan Inouye was a young boy in Waikiki in these golden years, a budding tenor saxophone and clarinet player interested in medicine. He remembers:

"Waikiki was a special paradise. You saw beautiful people, elegant people, men with turbans, women with flowery gowns. I saw Shirley Temple there sitting on the shoulder of Duke Kahanamoku. She was the darling of the world. Hollywood actors and actresses were all over The Royal — limousines, great music.

I used to surf at what was then called Gray's Beach, between the Royal and the Halekulani. We weren't permitted to surf at the Royal. That was for the top tourists and the top beachboys.

Then the beachboys — one was Steamboat and the other was Blue Makua — saw me surfing. One of them said, 'Come. Wanna work?' I said, 'Certainly.'

'We got some poor ones here. We'll give 'em to you. Ten cents an hour.'

Ten cents an hour was good money. I could go to a movie for ten cents, get two hamburgers for ten cents.

I would run down to Waikiki as soon as school was over and serve my apprenticeship with the older beachboys. Mostly they were Hawaiians, without organization or written regulations, but they operated an impenetrable closed shop.

I had this huge, heavy board. I'd place the tourists on it, wait for a wave to come in, and push them forward. Then I'd get the board, paddle it back to the breakers, put them on again, and push it toward the beach.

It didn't last long — one summer for something like four weeks. On the fourth week I was injured. While I was turning around waiting for a wave to come in, a wave from the front hit my board, and the board hit my head. I went unconscious temporarily. It's a good thing the tourists had the presence of mind to pick me up, put me on the board, and take me back in. That was the last time. I went home with a huge bump on my head. I don't know who he was, but he saved my life." [9]

President John F. Kennedy and U.S. Senator Daniel K. Inouye.

The Hawaiian beachboys represented the melting pot of Hawaiʻi's many cultures. As handsome athletes, they attracted more than a little attention from visitors of all stripes and ages, and by treating everyone equally and fairly, they established Waikiki as a place where people could ignore race and class and simply be friends. It was inevitable that visiting ladies were among their many admirers, romance being one of Waikiki's more available commodities. The friendships beachboys created with young, old, male, or female, white or otherwise, quietly showed the way past the racial biases still troubling mainland American culture.

Cary Grant with Sarge Kahanamoku.

Actress Deborah Kerr on a memorable canoe ride with Steamboat.

Crooner Bing Crosby in 1936 with beachboys (from left) Pua Kealoha, Chick Daniels and Joe Minor.

BEACHBOY DAYS — BY GRADY TIMMONS

A full century has passed since the beachboy first emerged onto the world stage, a product of the revival of Hawaiian water sports and the advent of tourism at Waikiki. Today this maverick profession still survives, but its golden, defining years were the decade leading up to the Second World War.

Like Waikiki itself, the beachboy came of age with the opening of The Royal Hawaiian in 1927. The Royal made the world take notice, transforming Waikiki into a seasonal rite of the rich and famous. The castlelike hostelry stood front and center on Waikiki Beach with pink stucco walls and more than 800 palm trees. Its guest register read like the cast of a blockbuster Hollywood movie. Behind The Royal Hawaiian lay a quiet residential and agricultural Waikiki, where flowers bloomed and palms swayed against the sky.

"Waikiki at that time was a very healing place," recalled Michael Mullahey, whose father Bill founded the Waikiki Beach Patrol under the auspices of the Outrigger Canoe Club. "You would come there because you instinctively knew that's where you needed to be if you wanted to rest, if you needed to get well. The waters were beneficent, the breezes were soothing, the whole vibration of the place was something that just drew you in. The people who came there really experienced relaxation, and in the beachboys they found a group of men who were funny, sharing, open, kind."

For the rich, the special appeal of the beachboy was that he did not have a hidden agenda. He served as a kind of all-purpose ambassador and a visitor's invaluable link to Waikiki. The late Chris Cusack, who came to Waikiki in 1927 and whose father was a dockside reporter and friend of writer Jack London, recalled that the beachboy was a one-man tourist bureau — a combination surfing instructor and social director who provided visitors with that unique island welcome known as "aloha."

In late afternoons, beachboys serenaded along the shore with their guitars and ukuleles. In the evenings, they performed in the hotels and at popular Waikiki nightclubs, where they were the life of the party. "There was a definite 'in' feeling the tourists got with the beachboys," Cusack said. "I suppose it was like going to Spain and meeting the matadors. The beachboys were very colorful and talented, and extremely loyal."

At Waikiki, the rich played hard and spent big, and in their own way were as eccentric as the beachboys they hung out with. There was Major Douglas King and his wife, Ruth, who came by ship from England to the East Coast, by train to the West Coast, and then by ship to Waikiki. The Kings brought their own china and silverware and stayed at The Royal Hawaiian in a double-suite with two maids and a pair of dogs. Bill Kahanamoku was their beachboy.

There was Chris Holmes, heir to the Fleischmann Yeast fortune, who installed surfboard gates at his Queen's Surf estate in Waikiki and whose family bought Coconut Island on the windward side of O'ahu, stocking it with monkeys, chimpanzees, an elephant, a shark pond, a cannon, and a yacht that came equipped with a bowling alley. Holmes liked to pal around with Chick Daniels and Pua Kealoha.

Frank Sinatra and Ava Gardner go for a canoe ride during their honeymoon at Waikiki in 1953. Sitting behind them are Chicago mobster Sam Giancana and his wife, plus Gene "Tarzan" Smith and Charlie Lambert. Giancana was the victim of a gangland slaying in 1975, just prior to testifying before the U.S. Congress.

And there was Doris Duke, the world's wealthiest woman, who built Shangri-la, a $2 million fantasy retreat at Diamond Head's Black Point. Her estate had fountains and waterfalls; chattering monkeys; gold, green, and red parrots and parakeets; and hundreds of cats. The Kahanamoku clan and Doris Duke were close friends.

Not surprisingly, the beachboys reaped many benefits from these relationships. As a measure of their friendship, the rich frequently took the beachboys with them on trips abroad. An obituary noting the death of Tough Bill Keaweamahi in 1955 revealed that he had been taken around the world seven times.

There were, of course, other benefits. William Clarke, a Montana copper magnate, paid for the educations of Olympic beachboy swimmers Pua Kealoha and Sam Kahanamoku. Doris Duke gave Sam a house. Freckles Lyons, beachboy for playboy millionaire George Vanderbilt, got the down payment for his house from the scion's family.

Cruise ships, boat days, and stateroom parties — all were part of a beachboy's daily existence. For many, leaving such a lifestyle was never easy. For the generation of beachboy Harry Robello it took a declaration of war. "If not for the war, I think not one beachboy would have left," he said. "I doubt it." The golden years — the sun, the surf, the parties, the associations with rich men and beautiful women — were just too good.

G.T.

Top left: Doris Duke is believed to be the girl surfing in the foreground.
Above: Doris Duke at Shangri-la with Sam and David Kahanamoku (wearing a hat).
Left: Major and Mrs. Douglas King of London were among the first ones to register at the Royal Hawaiian when it opened on February 1, 1927.

Amid a boom in visitors, Japan's invasion of China in 1937 and Germany's blitzkrieg into Poland in 1939 brought the likelihood of war into clear focus even in distant Waikiki. The U.S. military beefed up forces in Hawai'i, fortified the coastline with concrete bunkers and gun emplacements, trained a local guard, and rehearsed using searchlights in the event of night air raids. The Pacific Fleet increased in size and capability, and the Army even put in a newfangled, top secret device called radar to warn of approaching aircraft.

On the evening of Saturday, December 6, 1941 military officers were having a Christmas party at The Royal Hawaiian. Offshore a Japanese submarine hovered close enough to hear the music. According to hula legend "Tootsie" Notley: "It was a beautiful ball. I was one of the solo dancers at that thing. And I danced, and oh, I tell you, that place was just crawling with military. All the officers, big guns, of the Army, Navy, Marines at the Royal — all getting drunk."

On the morning of December 7, Waikiki residents were shocked when an anti-aircraft shell suddenly exploded near Ala Wai Boulevard, and churchgoers exiting St. Augustine's across from Waikiki Beach heard distant booms, then saw smoke rising from the Japanese surprise attack on Pearl Harbor.

Honolulu Star-Bulletin 1st EXTRA

(Associated Press by Transpacific Telephone)

WAR!

SAN FRANCISCO, Dec. 7.—President Roosevelt announced this morning that Japanese planes had attacked Manila and Pearl Harbor.

OAHU BOMBED BY JAPANESE PLANES

Explosion of the *U.S.S. Arizona* at Pearl Harbor.

Tanks rumble past The Royal Hawaiian on Kalakaua.

Anti-aircraft gunnery in the middle of a pineapple field.

CHAPTER 6

Waikiki Goes to War

It's what you learn after you know it all that counts.
John Wooden

The attack on Pearl Harbor turned life on sleepy O'ahu topsy turvy. The military declared martial law just after 4 PM on Sunday, December 7, 1941. Tourists were loaded on the first boat for home, and anti-invasion barricades brought the reality of war to the beach. The military took control of The Royal Hawaiian for a rest and recreation center, but not before The Royal's manager — responding to a temporary ban on alcohol — carried all the spirits in the place down to the wine cellar, cemented over the door and disguised it as a false pillar.

Certain that another attack would follow, the military issued identity cards and gas masks, and required all to have them when in public. Four months later in March of 1942, two Japanese seaplanes refueled from subs, then attacked O'ahu. Lost in clouds over the island, one dropped bombs in the sea off Pearl Harbor, and the other dropped several into the forest on Tantalus, a ridge above Manoa Valley and Waikiki. Though no one was injured, the military hushed up news of the raid.

Martial law meant censorship of letters, phone calls, radio broadcasts, newspapers, and magazines. The government set work hours and wages and required non-essential businesses to alter production for the war effort. Gasoline, meat, butter, eggs, tires, nylon stockings, and later liquor were all rationed.

The government also controlled housing and rents and required homes, businesses, and cars to meet night time blackout regulations. Servicemen doubled and quadrupled up in their rooms, and the bright lights of Waikiki disappeared behind blackout curtains. [1]

The military Governor set and strictly enforced a curfew, and in a sweeping change that led to several appeals to the U.S. Supreme Court, the military courts now tried all criminal cases whatever the offense, with over ninety percent of the accused found guilty. [2] Military officers with little or no legal training became the judges. U.S. Senator Dan Inouye recalls that these 'judges' — with .45 caliber pistols on their hips — routinely gave those convicted of lesser offenses a choice of punishments: a $25 fine, or a pint of blood for the war effort.

Sen. Inouye also recalls what happened to his family's brand new radio, a Christmas present they had saved for.

"The military government of Hawai'i issued an order saying that if you have radios that can get shortwave broadcasts, you must report that.

The wartime blackout and curfew did not stop people from having a good card game (note the flashlight).

Disguised in camouflage paint, Aloha Tower witnesses the debarkation of a contingent of WACs.

A sentinel stands guard on Waikiki Beach

'Iolani Palace gets wrapped in barbed wire fortification, circa 1941.

So we reported that immediately, and a few days later two men dressed in dark suits came up.

'Where's your radio?'

We took it out, and one took out a screwdriver and began to open up the back. So my dad said, 'May I help you unscrew this?'

'Oh no. Get away! Get away!'

Then he shoved his hand in and just started pulling out the wiring and the tubes. Now you could have fixed that radio just by clipping a few wires to take out the shortwave section and still had a good radio. So my father without batting an eye said, 'Let me help you.'

We had an outdoor fireplace where we heated water and cooked rice, and he got the little hatchet that we used to cut kindling, and proceeded toward the radio. The men suddenly went for their .45s. They thought they were going to get attacked.

But he said, 'No, no,' went up to the radio, and in my presence, just smashed it to smithereens. He said, 'Here it is now. You satisfied?'

The two men just left." [3]

The U.S. government suspiciously eyed the 158,000 Americans of Japanese ancestry (AJAs) in Hawai'i's population. Despite being citizens and taxpayers, AJAs had to wear a patch designating their ethnicity on their clothing, and had to stay clear of government buildings. While across America AJAs were interned and had their property seized, the military government in Hawai'i responded to public pressure and was far less severe. Of an AJA population of some 150,000 people, they selectively culled just 525 community leaders, who were interned along with 976 Japanese nationals. [4]

Hawaii ★ PARADISE OF THE PACIFIC

U.S. CAFE

Welcome TO THE PERSONNEL OF THE U.S. ARMY, NAVY & MARINES

1034 BETHEL ST. HONOLULU, HAWAII

CLOSE COVER BEFORE STRIKING

Leaders of the Japanese community were interned in camps like this one on Sand Island.

In August of 1936 President Roosevelt had written the Chief of Naval Operations that "in the event of trouble" with Japan, the U.S. would need to remove to concentration camps any Japanese Americans on Oʻahu known to have had contact with visiting Japanese ships, i.e., Roosevelt had already decided that in response to a Japanese attack on Oʻahu, some of Hawaiʻi's AJA citizens would lose their constitutional rights. After the Pearl Harbor attack, Secretary of the Navy Knox insisted that AJAs posed threats to the war effort, despite the FBI and Attorney General Biddle indicating to the President that there was no evidence to support that claim. [5]

Despite unfounded official suspicions about AJA loyalties, Hawaiʻi's war effort relied on AJA talents in the shipyards, for construction, and for a variety of war-related jobs, including work in Waikiki. As military governor of the islands, General Emmons understood: incarcerating over 150,000 people would require more resources than the war-strapped U.S. had to spend — and it would be wrong. Emmons realized as well that putting 37% of Hawaiʻi's population in camps would

destroy civilian morale and devastate the economy of the islands just when a healthy Hawaiʻi was vital to the war effort. [6] Despite facing a wholesale denial of their constitutional rights, AJAs would prove themselves loyal Americans in ways that Hawaiʻi and the nation could never forget.

With the huge influx of GIs and civilian workers, money flooded into the wartime economy of Oʻahu. Besides trying to keep up with the demand for military housing, builders had to create living quarters for the tens of thousands civilian workers flowing into Civilian Housing Area 3 (CHA3) near Pearl Harbor. The instant town housed 12,000 men, including hard hat divers, who raised four sunken battleships, and civilian workers repairing damaged vessels in the shipyards. For these men, working seven days a week, a trip off base meant a ride on a crowded bus or an expensive cab fare, a curfew, and a blackout requiring an early return. But tens of thousands managed to make their way to that fabled paradise, Waikiki Beach.

Hawaiʻi's population swelled as it became the stopover for over a million servicemen, American boys on their way to some of the most intense land and sea battles in the history of warfare.

The Royal Hawaiian, the Moana, and Fort DeRussy became major recreation centers for soldiers, sailors, engineers, and civilian workers. The Navy leased The Royal for $17,500 a month to house submariners in from war patrols — all volunteers in the war's most dangerous job. [11] Lonely men far from home responded to warm Hawaiian aloha and mobbed recreation dances and USOs, where local girls danced with them under strict supervision. At Fort DeRussy the Maluhia ballroom held up to 1200 people, but occasionally 10,000 men arrived hoping to dance with one of the 100 to 300 local girls who volunteered their time.

When they weren't busy serving as air raid wardens or home guards, Waikiki's residents opened their doors to lonely

Hula dancer entertains some Navy men.

The famous 100th Battalion and 442nd "Go For Broke" at the heart of Europe's bloodiest battlefronts.

AJA soldiers induction ceremony in Honolulu, circa 1944.

servicemen far from their own homes. Waikiki bandleader Johnny Noble wrote *Remember Pearl Harbor*, a song that became a patriotic anthem nationwide. Artie Shaw and other major musical talents performed at The Breakers, and every month some 50,000 military personnel and civilian workers would find their way to jazz and big band swing music in Waikiki, day or night. [12]

Hawaiian citizens showed their patriotism by spending nearly four times as much on war bonds as mainland Americans. AJAs created their own 100th Battalion and the famous 442nd "Go For Broke" Regiment, sustaining heavy casualties and covering themselves with glory fighting in Italy and across the European front. As the 21st century opened generations later, a monument in the nation's capital, memorialized the achievements and losses of AJA soldiers and the U.S. government's tragic internment of AJA citizens.

President Roosevelt arrived in July 1944 and over the next several days worked with Admiral Nimitz and General MacArthur at millionaire Chris Holmes' beautiful Queens Surf estate in the shadow of Diamond Head. The setting provided the right backdrop for FDR to settle some serious disputes between the Navy's Admiral Nimitz and the Army's General MacArthur over their strategies for the remainder of the Pacific war.

More than anything that had preceded it, WWII linked Hawai'i — and with it Waikiki — to American culture, American history, and the dominant themes of WWII America — sacrifice and working toward a common purpose. When Japan was defeated in 1945, local celebrations went on for days, while back in the continental United States, Waikiki had become a household word.

A group of Leathernecks and nurses enjoys a very traditional pleasure of the Islands, the luau.

Paradise Engraving   SAILORS' SWEETHEARTS OF OLDEN DAYS   By a Visiting Cartoonist

War production required some notable forms of specialized labor. As tens of thousands of men arrived on Oʻahu, prostitution was outlawed in Waikiki, where one episode in a hotel had created a hubbub. But prostitution flourished downtown on Hotel Street, where two hundred and fifty "entertainers" paid a dollar annual fee for a license to serve men in some fifteen brothels. Hawaiʻi's "entertainers" wore anklets to signify their trade, and organized their sexual commerce as a kind of assembly line. After standing in lines that sometimes circled the block, clients had a bare three minutes to take care of their sexual needs and paid three dollars for the favor. Nearby military medics supplied hygiene. [7]

The military had agreed with the chief of police to allow prostitution around Hotel Street. When a few of these hard-working ladies decided to live away from the job and go where they pleased in their off hours, police dealt with them harshly, beating them and returning them to Hotel Street and Chinatown. The prostitutes complained of the police brutality to the military Provost Marshall, and when they got no justice, the most unusual labor dispute in American history erupted.

Although they had no union, Hotel Street's prostitutes went on strike for three weeks and picketed the police department headquarters (where the MPs also centered their operations). Under martial law, the ladies hadn't had much choice when the military set their prices. Now, given the immense demand for them among servicemen and civilian workers, the ladies of the night believed they had an effective bargaining position. Prostitutes picketing a police station did little to create public confidence in the authorities, and the strike was crippling military morale.

Moreover, local police, long accustomed to getting favors from madams, hated to see their side income disappear. Acknowledging the considerable value of these women to the war effort, authorities quietly caved in and let them roam or live where they wanted to. [8]

Eventually several madams bought houses in nice neighborhoods. One of them was said to have told the neighbors the nature of her work, then sold back immediately for a higher price when neighbors feared for their property values. Another received a commendation from the Secretary of the Treasury for selling over $100,000 in war bonds. [9] And a third paid income taxes of $338,000 in 1943. In September of 1944, with the Japanese threat abated, local citizens pressured the authorities into shutting down all of the brothels. [10]

CHAPTER 7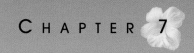

ANATOMY OF A BOOM

The future is not what it used to be.
Paul Valery

The headline read, "Can Lovely Waikiki Stage A Comeback?" and the question needed answers. With the end of hostilities, easy money from servicemen and war workers disappeared abruptly, and Hawai'i found herself in a slump. On the mainland, as factories retooled and GIs sought jobs, America wasn't thinking about vacations in balmy Honolulu. For a couple of years at least, Honolulu wasn't ready for them either.

Painting by Lt. Hunter Woods, U.S. Merchant Marine Cadet Corps, depicting a rescue operation by the *Monterey*, former Matson liner, converted into a troopship.

Matson's luxurious white ships had been commandeered, gutted and refitted to carry troops. Reversing the process was outrageously expensive. (The *Lurline* cost $7.9 million to build in 1933. Thirteen years later, it took $20 million to return her to original condition — only about 25% of which was paid by the government.) Hotels, too, had been battered by the wartime trade. But as the barbed wire along the beach came down, Waikiki looked in the mirror and recognized herself — same old palms dancing in the tradewinds, same clear crystal waters, same fleets of clouds sailing slowly across sunny skies. Musicians came back to work, and beachboys, some of them veterans now, returned to their old haunts. No one realized that the lazy, late 1940's would later feel like the pause before a whirlwind.

On April Fools Day, 1946, Sadao Hikida was on the beach at 6 AM and got the scare of his life: "I looked out and saw the water receding rapidly toward the horizon with the reef all protruding. Not realizing it was the sign of a tidal wave ... I ran into the ocean looking for fishes ... I was about fifty to seventy yards out when I looked toward the horizon. I saw the wave like it was boiling, and getting bigger and bigger, and heading toward shore. I ran as fast as I could ... just barely made it to shore and over the wall when the first wave hit land. I ran into the hotel (Moana) and told people that a tidal

wave had occurred, but they didn't believe me because it was April Fools Day. I took the elevator to the sixth floor and watched the tidal wave come in. Hardly any damage ... the waves washed up to Kalakaua Avenue, and loose boards and canoes washed out to sea."

Fortunately the tsunami — which had caused horrific loss of life and property in Hilo on the Big Island of Hawai'i — fell short of damaging Waikiki. They already had enough to contend with.

Some 600 construction workers hammered, nailed, painted and refurbished The Royal Hawaiian, repairing the havoc wrought by more than three years of Navy men. Frank Palmer was the project supervisor for the $2 million job: "The sailors were not kind to the hotel. They would pry off the mosquito screens and sail them out the windows into the courtyard, start campfires on the carpet and throw knives at the woodwork. We had a horrendous job restoring the hotel to its luxury status."

The Royal Hawaiian re-opened for business with a gala affair on February 1, 1947 — twenty years to the day of her original opening. By, then, Frank Palmer was chief engineer for Matson's hotels. He recollects: "One morning, Speed Garris, the hotel's chief of security, came to me with Bert Trajillo, who was in charge of wines and liquors, and asked me to come down to the basement with them. It's dark down there, with pillars and long tunnels, and when we came to a nondescript wall with dirt piled against it, Speed drew a big square with chalk on it and said, 'I want a door right here.'

"We started jackhammering the wall. It was concrete two feet thick and took a couple days. I was hammering this wall, surrounded by security men. I finally broke through, and Speed reached in and flicked on a light switch. I couldn't believe my eyeballs—there was a huge room filled with vintage wines, expensive liquors and champagne. It had been the old wine cellar, and just before turning over the keys of the hotel to the Navy, they emptied all the bars and sealed their contents, with a wall that looked just like a part of the foundation. The champagne crates had rotted in the dampness, leaving bottles stacked on top of each other more than 4 feet high! The submariners never knew it was there, or they'd have torn the hotel apart brick by brick looking for it. They spent the war — like all of us did — drinking Five Islands Gin, which everyone used to say was brewed in a bathtub on Tuesday and being imbibed on Wednesday."

Airplanes had become commonplace and far more reliable during WWII. Passenger planes now reached Hawai'i in twelve hours, Douglas DC 6s and 7s replacing the old Boeing seaplanes. By 1950, 45,000 visitors appeared, an amazing leap of 35% in a year. [2] Air travel, once a luxury reserved for the very wealthy, was becoming affordable for everyone.

Waikiki in this era still had a sleepy quality. When the aging Waikiki Bowling Alley adjoining the Moana Hotel was torn down, the ancient *pohaku* stones, vanished since the 1920's, appeared as part of its foundations. They were returned to Kuhio Beach and enclosed as a revered part of Waikiki's history. Entertainer Boyce Rodrigues recalls working with the musicians at The Royal Hawaiian who scheduled their breaks to coincide with the evening mullet run offshore, hustling out to catch fish before returning to perform the next set. There were new songs to sing, and new and familiar singers to perform them. During a few winter nights in Lansing, Michigan, performing with E.K. Fernandez' Extravaganza, Andy Cummings felt the pull of Hawai'i and wrote the timeless lyric and haunting melody, *Waikiki —* *"For you my poor heart is yearning ... Magic beside the sea ... magic of Waikiki."*

In the early fifties, Arthur Godfrey had an enormous national audience for his weekly radio and TV shows. He sang, interviewed people, acted as talent scout for new entertainers, and played his 'ukulele. There Godfrey was, on TV, clad in an aloha shirt, giving the audience lessons in how to strum. Sales of ukes again soared into the millions, and Waikiki caught the national spotlight on CBS when Godfrey broadcast his shows from Waikiki beach. [3]

In 1954 the musical trio of Martin Denny, Arthur Lyman, and Augie Colon created a new exotic tropical sound with bird calls and vibraphone. Soon radio stations all over the world were playing *Quiet Village* from the album *Exotica*, and Arthur Lyman went on to compose his big hit *Taboo*. [4]

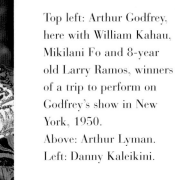

Top left: Arthur Godfrey, here with William Kahau, Mikilani Fo and 8-year old Larry Ramos, winners of a trip to perform on Godfrey's show in New York, 1950.
Above: Arthur Lyman.
Left: Danny Kaleikini.

HOTELS AND HOLO HOLO FOR EVERYONE

Hawai'i was on the map for entertainment headliners everywhere — Duke Ellington, Billy Holiday, Louis Armstrong, Mose Allison, June Christie, Benny Carter — and at the Waikiki Tavern right on the beach, a young comic named Lenny Bruce was performing.

With statehood and a visitor boom, the Waikiki Shell booked national acts — Johnny Cash, Ricky Nelson, and Hawai'i's own Dave Guard and Bob Shane of the Kingston Trio, all playing in Kapi'olani Park. Elvis Presley played the old stadium, then two years later showed his love for the islands as well as his patriotism when he performed a benefit concert that generated thousands of dollars to complete the *U.S.S. Arizona* Memorial.

Hotel keeper Roy Kelley saw the commercial future of making Waikiki available to everyone. Waikiki's earlier days had meant elegance, grace, and fatter wallets. From the day Kelley opened the affordable Edgewater in 1950, it sold out. Waikiki was now available to a much broader spectrum of travelers, and businesses responded with affordable restaurants, bars, and shops. [5]

Legend has it that when Kelley opened a restaurant in the Edgewater, he was getting ready for a long off-island trip. He gave the restaurant manager a cigar box with thousands of dollars in it and told him: put all of the receipts back into the box, and pay for all of the restaurant's supplies and staff out of the box. If the box runs out of money, close the place. [6] Graduate schools of business loved the Kelley example of practical management.

JETS AND TURF DISPUTES

In July of 1959, jets began to arrive, and Waikiki was now four and a half hours away from California. Tourism jumped 43% that year, then another 23% the next year. [7]

In the mid 1950's an esthetic planner had advanced the notion of realigning part of Waikiki's main street, Kalakaua Avenue, towards the mountains — *mauka*. The thought was to create a park which, except for then existing hotels, would extend from the street to

the beach. It was a grand idea, for it meant everyone passing through Waikiki would have a view of the sea and the sand. It was deemed unaffordable.

In the 1960's developers wanted to build high rise hotels and condominiums along the slopes of Diamond Head. In the ensuing unpleasantries, City Council hearings were held, friendships were lost, and money flowed to achieve political and economic purpose. In the final inning, however, the forces of esthetics and environmental protection saved Diamond Head from disappearing behind a hodge podge of high rises. [8]

STATEHOOD

In August of 1959, sixty-one years after annexation, Hawai'i became the 50th state. Citizens took to dancing in the streets, and military planes and ships fired flares off Waikiki to celebrate the occasion. Arrivals at Honolulu Airport leapt from two planes a day to twenty. People were pouring in so fast that the state began building a new airport, a job which would see five governors come and go until it was completed, thirty-five years later.

Visitors numbers continued to soar, creating an obvious problem: Waikiki didn't have enough rooms. Airlines and hotel keepers held emergency meetings, and a building boom unlike anything in island history began to reconfigure Waikiki. In 1960, two thousand more hotel rooms were under construction.

Statehood celebrations went on for days and days, with dancing in the streets. Top right: It was long assumed that Hawai'i would be admitted ahead of Alaska, hence the "49th State" record label.

101

In the film, *Waikiki, In the Wake of Dreams*, columnist Eddie Sherman remembers comic Lenny Bruce:

"Lenny was at the Orchid Room at the Waikiki Tavern in the late 1950's. There weren't that many showrooms in Waikiki then, and whenever a comic came to Honolulu, I made it point to see the act. Having done battle on the stage myself, I had a lot of aloha for comics, and felt they were my people.

Lenny was young, handsome, and cleancut, married to a stripper named Honey Harlow who was featured in a lot of clubs. Although Lenny was really bright, he worked with a standard type comedy act of impressions and jokes and songs. He was a very likable guy, always friendly and accommodating. I spent many nights at his show, and later hung out with him along with Aku, Hawai'i's top disk jockey then. I remember one night Lenny was exceptionally good and got a great reception from the audience. For his final bow, he came out stark naked, with only a black derby over his privates. He just stood there smiling as the applause continued, then finally said, "Thank you so much!" and extended both of his arms.

That audience got to see the birth of the legendary Lenny Bruce just beginning to emerge from his cocoon . . . right here in Waikiki."

A VILLAGE FOR WAIKIKI

Industrialist Henry Kaiser arrived in 1955, at age 77 energized about pushing Hawai'i's development. He created the suburb of Hawai'i Kai and then acquired 25 acres in Waikiki, including the old Niumalu Hotel near Kalia Road. Putting in thatched roof huts, he built the famous Hilton Hawaiian Village.

He added a beachside Little League baseball park and put together teams of local kids who needed uniforms, gloves, and a place to play. Given its location on Waikiki Beach, people remarked that the kids' baseball park probably had the same real estate value as that of Yankee Stadium. The ballpark soon gave way to hotel towers and a parking garage. [9] In need of a show-room and venue for conventions, Kaiser built a Buckminster Fuller geodesic dome, which went up virtually overnight. Kaiser's Village became the biggest resort in Waikiki. With Benny Kalama as musical director and the legendary Alfred Apaka singing at the Tapa Room, it had no trouble drawing visitors. Kaiser had tapped the American dream of Waikiki as paradise. With performers such as Apaka, Arthur Lyman, Boyce Rodrigues, and Renee Paulo, plus the popular new TV series *Hawaiian Eye* using the Hilton as a set, his vision was a great success.

Alfred Apaka

Right: Henry J. Kaiser aboard his catamaran.

HOLLYWOOD AGAIN

Hollywood rediscovered Waikiki in a big way from the 1950's through the 1980's. 20th Century Fox's *Adventures in Paradise* series with Gardner McKay sent out weekly black and white TV images of the south seas and the TV series *Hawaiian Eye* debuted with Robert Conrad and Connie Stevens. Then the Academy Award-winning feature *From Here To Eternity* put Hawai'i back on the map.

Burt Lancaster and Deborah Kerr in the Oscar winning feature movie, *From Here To Eternity*.

Films such as *Gidget Goes Hawaiian* and Elvis Presley's *Blue Hawai'i* relied on proven formulas for box office success: stereotypical Hawaiians still strumming the 'ukulele and beautiful women dancing the hula. But now Hollywood capitalized on two crazes of the era — rock 'n roll and surfing. Then came Leonard Freeman's long-running hit television series *Hawaii 5-0*, which generated top audience ratings that marketed Waikiki and the islands worldwide. By the time Tom Selleck's

Lee Marvin, star of the *M Squad* TV show, poses with (left) Leimoni Buchanon (Miss Kaua'i 1961) and Marnelyn Buchanon (right-Miss Kaua'i 1962).

103

Clockwise from top
left: Jane Russell in
*The Revolt of Mamie
Stover*, Jack Lord,
Tom Selleck and
Gardner McKay.

detective series *Magnum P.I.* inherited 5-0's place in the primetime television of the 1980's, everyone in the western industrialized world had heard of and seen Waikiki. Hotel keepers in Rio or Cannes might argue about it, but Waikiki was the most famous beach in the world, and Hollywood had contributed substantially to its mythology.

Between 1953 and 1962, at the *ewa* (western) edge of Waikiki, the Dillingham Corporation dredged out a yacht harbor near the mouth of the Ala Wai Canal, trading its labors for the sand and coral that filled in the first half of Ala Moana Shopping Center. [10] While it seemed a bit incongruous to find a shopping center of such huge scale in the central Pacific, the complex would boast that it was — at least temporarily — the largest shopping center in the world. Part of its demand came from Waikiki visitors. On its *makai* (seaward) side, a huge peninsula of dredged coral became "Magic Island," a park marking a border for Waikiki.

When a million visitors arrived in 1962, the visitor industry hardly paused to admire the milestone. The twenty-five story Foster Towers was rising across from Kuhio Beach, setting off a controversy about ruining the view of Diamond Head, but as hotel owners saw it, the room for visitors lay above Waikiki. It was either build into it, or watch the visitors go elsewhere. In the midst of debate about construction, one warm August night the U.S. military set off a hydrogen bomb 800 miles south of O'ahu on Johnson Island. The huge glowing cloud lit up the distant night sky off Waikiki, reminding everyone that paradise was now part of the Cold War.

Above: Unveiling in 1959 of the Ala Moana Shopping Center model. Below: Aerial showing the sheer size of the Ala Moana Shopping Center, and the yacht harbor.

QUEENS SURF

Part of Waikiki's attraction now lay in the variety of great entertainment and food available there. From one end of Waikiki to the other you could find local folks and visitors enthusiastically dining at Kau Kau Korner, Swanky Frankies, The Tropics, showman Jack Cione's Forbidden City, Hot Dog Annies and The Tahitian Lanai. More elegant dining was available from high-end hotel restaurants, the kimono-clad waitresses at Canlis or the posh French cuisine at Michel's. Don The Beachcomber's offered funky tropical decor and multi-hued drinks, while everyone crowded into the legendary Barefoot Bar at Queens Surf for great entertainment and the best "people watching."

By day Queens Surf was a favorite local beach with a bar and hamburger joint, but by night, you dined on prime rib or followed the painted footprints upstairs to Queens Surf's Barefoot Bar, the hottest night spot in Waikiki. With cop-turned-musician Sterling Mossman as personable emcee, Mahi Beamer, Eddie Kamae's Sons of Hawai'i, and the legendary *kiho alo* (Hawaiian slack key guitar) artist Gabby Pahinui performed. In typical Hawaiian style, local and visiting musicians often sat in.

Don Ho tells the story this way: "I got a call to go to Queens Surf to take Sterling Mossman's place. He was going on vacation. Queens Surf was the heart and soul of Waikiki at that point, the first real local hang-out. We had the worst band — I was not really a musician, just play-ing the organ amateurishly. Raymond Kahola played uke and broke strings all the time, but he sang like an angel, and the fire dancer was our bass player . . . we had no intention of anything except surviving, but we packed 'em in." [13]

Among the local talents at the Barefoot Bar was a young man named Kui Lee, songwriter, singer, and the pride of Honolulu's Hawaiian homestead Papakolea. Lee wrote both lively and poignant music that resonated with locals and visitors alike. Don Ho's record-ing of Lee's ballad *I'll Remember You* hit the charts across the coun-try, and made both of them hugely popular. With Lee's early death, Hawai'i lost an original poet whose artistry tapped the feelings of Hawaiian hearts. Don Ho puts it succinctly, "Kui was a genius."

Ex-Air Force pilot Don Ho had been drawing crowds at his moth-er's small establishment, Honey's. After short gigs at Queens Surf and the lounge at Hilton Hawaiian Village, he became a huge draw at a new hot spot, Dukes, in the International Market Place. He notes "Duke Kahanamoku was the role model for being a Hawaiian, a true gentleman. I ended up there because Duke said, 'Don, come to Dukes.' [14] The true Hawaiian flavor of his show and his interplay with an audience led Don Ho directly to the top. He was soon appearing on national television with Bob Hope, Dinah Shore, and Johnny Carson's Tonite Show, top TV shows of the era. He rapidly evolved into Hawai'i's best recognized entertain-er, and remains today, a source of encouragement and inspiration to young artists of Hawai'i.

DUKE KAHANAMOKU

Long before his name appeared on a nightclub, a surfing meet, and a line of sportswear, Duke had become the ambassador of Waikiki. Quite simply, he was the one everyone wanted to meet. Duke was honored on the popular national TV series *This Is Your Life*, hosted by Ralph Edwards. Columnist Eddie Sherman laughs that a similar tribute was later put together at The Hilton Hawaiian Village. "Duke was given the place of honor in a chair on the stage. When the lights went down, the audience watched Duke's life unfold before them on film, but when the lights came up and the applause rose, there was Duke, asleep in his chair.[15] True to form, Duke was simply demonstrating that fame needn't get in the way of what mattered in life.

Duke died in 1968. Off Waikiki's shoreline where he spent his youth, Duke was given the biggest beachboy funeral in history.

Clockwise from top left: Duke with Danny Kaye; with Babe Ruth and his wife; with Charlie Chaplin and Paulette Goddard; canoes at Duke's beachboy funeral; with John Wayne on movie set; with Mary Pickford, Arthur Benaglia and Douglas Fairbanks; with Groucho Marx; Duke's widow Nadine (in white) with Arthur Godfrey follow Rev. Abraham Akaka carrying Duke's ashes.

107

The Surf Rider
HAWAII

SURFING

Surfing legend Fred Hemmings observed, "Waikiki was the cradle of surfing," but now surfing had become an entire culture that had gone worldwide, with Duke as its icon, and Hawai'i's water sportsmen its heroes. Hemmings, Jeff Hakman, Joey Cabell, and a host of other surfing champions turned professional, with well-engineered, lightweight foam surfboards, which were a far cry from Duke's huge redwood monsters.

In the 1960's someone added roller skate wheels to a small board, and across America Waikiki's ancient sport of kings swept the streets as skateboarding. In 1975 a talented young sailor named Robbie Naish sold his Hobie Cat to buy an early windsurfing rig, and a year later flipped and flew into the first of six consecutive world

championships. Soon there were professional windsurfing contests in Europe, and at the bend of the mighty Columbia River in Hood River, Oregon. In search of greater challenges, surfers realized that if you crossed a surfboard with a ski, and added fittings for boots, quite amazingly, you could surf the slopes on something called a snowboard. People riding boards — Waikiki's gift to the world.

Development continued to escalate. During the Vietnam War armed forces rest and recreation in Waikiki became a popular choice for military personnel, and by 1970, with the advent of jumbo jets that carried 400 passengers, state visitor counts jumped to 1.8 million, then quickly to over 3.2 million in 1976. More visitors meant more traffic, more potential for crime, and more demand on city services. On the beach at Waikiki, the sand grew crowded.

Aloha meant taking care of people, and security throughout the rapidly growing resort was remarkable. Beachboys kept an eye out for the safety of visitors, and the new Metro Squad of the Honolulu Police Department — plainclothes martial arts experts — did the same. [16]

The top recruit in his class, Larry Mehau accepts his HPD badge from Chief Dan Liu. Mehau soon went on to head the famed Metro Squad, where he emphasized weight training and martial arts. c. 1953.

IT WASN'T ALL BUSINESS

Like the Hawaiians of old, people in Waikiki didn't lack for imagination or energy when it came to enjoying sports or concocting good times. At the public course across the Ala Wai Canal, more golfers teed it up than at

any other course in America, sometimes getting in line for tee times at three AM. With its annual Kamehameha Day and Aloha Week parades, Waikiki had a regular flow of floats, grand marshals, marching bands, and *pa'u* riders *(women in traditional Hawaiian pa'u riding skirts)*. From its start in 1973, the Honolulu Marathon grew into one of the nation's largest. Like vast schools of fish, thousands of runners flowed through Waikiki in the pre-dawn hours, then struggled up the rise of Diamond Head and eventually finished at Kapi'olani Park.

Whatever the action ashore, athletes clearly had an ongoing love affair with the waters off Waikiki. The Diamond Head buoy marked the finish line for the biennial Transpac Yacht Race, sailing regattas plowed the waters offshore, and the Rough Water Swim left contestants stroking the length of the beach. With teams from all over the world, annual canoe races from Moloka'i finished at Waikiki.

Clusters of surfers still lined up for a series of breaks spanning over two miles of shoreline, and down by the Kapahulu seawall the bodyboarders continued their tradition of kamakazi rides in the shorebreak. On any late afternoon, canoes full of young athletes could be seen paddling against the sunset outside the reef.

By day the Kodak Hula Show offered Hawaiian music and hula in bright sunshine, perfect for exposing lots and lots of print, slide and movie film in yellow boxes. At night Waikiki was ablaze with the stars of Hawaiian music. Legendary entertainer Boyce Rodriques: "There was nothing to spend much on during the war, so afterwards everybody had plenty. Going down to Waikiki was fun in those days!"

Queens Surf was a huge hit. Entrepreneur Chinn Ho purchased it from Chris Holmes' estate and opened it before either The Royal or Moana had completed their postwar rebuilds, so competition was light. The City condemned the property, then turned around and leased it to restaurateur Spence Weaver. Sterling Mossman, a former H.P.D officer, was the headliner, but others who starred there until its unfortunate demolition in the early 70's included Mahi Beamer, Andy Cummings, the Kalama Brothers with Richard Kaui, and Varova Tiki.

The 50's and 60's were the high point for big Waikiki showrooms, and the trend continued. Headliners of the era who captivated audiences included (in alphabetical order): The Aliis, Johnny and Pua Almeida, Alfred Apaka, the Beamer Brothers, Jerry Byrd, the Brothers Cazimero, Sonny Chillingworth, Charles K.L. Davis, Loyal Garner, Louis Guererro, Al Harrington, Hilo Hattie, Don Ho, Dick Jenson, Haunani Kahalewai, Richard Kaui, Ed Kenney, Iva Kinimaka, The Krush, Kui Lee, Melveen Leed, Iolani Luahine, Bev Noa, Gabby Pahinui, Boyce Rodrigues, Marlene Sai, SOS (Society of Seven), The Surfers, Tihati, Emma Veary and Zulu.

Slowly, as the visitor mix changed, the showrooms closed to Hawaiian music. By the late 90's Waikiki offered visitors flamboyant magic shows and celebrity impersonators. As Hawaiian musicians left Waikiki, they were accompanied by the local audiences whose presence and enthusiasm had been a staple of Waikiki for generations.

Frank DeLima

The Brothers Cazimero and Peter Moon.

The Beamer Brothers —
Keola and Kapono.

A Trip Through Waikiki by the Numbers

Economics supplies only one view of the past, sometimes a rather dull, narrow, chart-ridden perspective. On the other hand, news of who gets what, when, and how usually has a place in our dreams of the good life. So don your economic glasses, if you will, and examine for a few moments what the story of dreamy Waikiki contributed to the dreams and awakenings of Hawai'i's residents in the latter part of the 20th century.

The gold rush in Waikiki saw development stretch out over thirty years. For the fifteen years following statehood, visitor counts doubled every four to six years. [17] With labor hard to find and unemployment rates hovering at some three percent, immigrants from the mainland and abroad piled in to fill visitor industry jobs. State population jumped 37% in just fifteen years, creating a housing shortage. [18] Much as sugar and pineapple had in the late 19th century, the successful visitor industry was adding to and changing Hawai'i's population. [19]

Pounding pile drivers, swinging construction cranes, and rumbling cement trucks appeared and disappeared regularly. Cottages and homes became hotels stretching skyward. The "Jungle" on the Diamond Head end of Waikiki — old wooden houses and two story apartments dating to the 1920's and 30's — was the last vestige of the past to vanish. [20] Jokers suggested that the construction crane was now the state bird. It seemed a simple proposition: either build enough rooms for visitors now, or lose the business. The only question seemed to be just where and how much more to build.

Waikiki was once more the breadbasket, now producing 18% of gross state product. [21] But when a population doubles as fast as it did in Waikiki, it suddenly needs twice as much of everything — food, water, sewers, transportation, energy, police and fire protection, trash pickup, laundry service, and, yes, even beach space. [22] Open space was disappearing in the rush, as were views of Diamond Head and the ocean. Perhaps even more importantly, some wondered if there were still enough Hawaiians to go around. After all, what makes Waikiki unique lies in its Hawaiian character. As the number of visitors vastly outnumbered the neighborhood's Hawaiians, the Waikiki experience was subtly diluted.

Still, the clear water, a place to flop on the beach, the tradewinds, ageless palms, and warm aloha were readily available. Visitors loved Waikiki and its magic, eloquent testimony that there was still a lot there to love.

Never had so many enjoyed so much from so little. The geography known as Waikiki is a spare 2.5 miles long by .75 of a mile wide. Absent Kapi'olani Park, it represents less than a square mile. But by the early 1980's it had some 28,000 hotel rooms with 50,000 visitors, and some 38,000 workers supplying goods and services. In the midst of this thriving visitor community lay a community of 20,000 permanent residents. [23] With 108,000 people in it daily, and more during high visitor season, Waikiki held 10% of everyone in the state in its tiny square mile, and to make that possible, people were stacked atop one another in high rises. Its 1980's population of more than 100,000 people per square mile qualified it as one of the most densely populated pieces of real estate in the world. [24]

To make sure people weren't also stacked atop one another on the beach, the sands of Waikiki were renewed and expanded repeatedly from the late 1930's through the 1970's. Beachfront stretching from Kuhio Beach to the Hilton Hawaiian Village could hold some 14,000 people, estimating a patch five feet by eight feet for each sunbather. [25] More visitors would inevitably require more beach space.

By the mid-1980's Waikiki had become an economic marvel admired the world over. Local folks ventured down to swim, surf, sun, watch surf meets, walk the beach, and go to restaurants, movies, and nightclubs there. Paddling teams practiced on the Ala Wai Canal in the late afternoon sun, and Kapiʻolani Park had its daily complement of joggers, tennis players, soccer teams, and softball games. But despite tens of thousands of permanent Waikiki residents and local people enjoying its charms, some felt that the crowded hotels and sheer number of visitors in the beachside community made it, at least psychologically, a place apart from the rest of Honolulu.

tors, but merchants and young people wanting first-hand experience with the American culture and economy into which Japan was busily selling its products. As the annual numbers of Japanese visitors increased to over a million and a half, businesses in Hawaiʻi rushed to accommodate their tastes.

In 1974 Japanese investor Kenji Osano recognized Waikiki's possibilities and purchased the Moana-Surfrider and Princess Kaʻiulani hotels. [26] A decade later, Osano acquired the majestic Royal Hawaiian and its beachmate, the Sheraton Waikiki. More and more affluent Japanese visitors arrived to splash at the beach and play Hawaiʻi's

JAPAN DISCOVERS AMERICA — IN WAIKIKI

Recognizing that development in Waikiki was reaching its physical limits, the City instituted a moratorium limiting further building there in the early 1980's — just as visitor demand took another leap. History was serving up another lesson in international trade. Japan's industrial economy was swelling so fast that Waikiki became the resort of choice for Japanese workers and professionals wanting a taste of paradise. The flow from Japan now included not only visi-

golf courses. Japanese weddings became part of Waikiki's economy, public signage appeared in Japanese, and in a decade Japanese spending amounted to some forty percent of all visitor revenues.

What happened next shows how history repeats its lessons. The sandalwood trade and provisions for whalers had attracted visitors and commerce to the islands in the early 19th century, but with sandalwood exhausted and petroleum replacing whale oil, mid-19th century visitor traffic had plummeted. Now events from far over the horizon once more shaped the fate of Waikiki.

As American music, movies, and clothes became popular in

Japan, Japanese manufacturers quietly seized 23% of automobile sales in the U.S. and took over the U.S. market for TV sets, video cassette recorders, and a host of electronic devices. With the balance of trade shifted heavily in Japan's favor, profits in dollars flowed into the coffers of Japanese businesses. Currency exchange rates left the dollar weak and the yen strong, making Hawai'i an easily affordable vacation for the Japanese.

Waikiki metamorphosed into an international resort on a scale no one had imagined possible, and King David Kalakaua's dream of close links with Japan came true. With an American recession

A YEN FOR PARADISE

There were success stories, but each suggested an economic bubble that couldn't swell much further. At one point, a shop in Waikiki's Royal Hawaiian Shopping Center was doing more dollars of business per square foot than any retail store in America, virtually all of it in sales to the Japanese. As the yen rapidly gained strength against the dollar, it had the effect of putting everything in America on sale to the Japanese at roughly half price. Japanese acquired more businesses in Waikiki, and tour buses full of visitors from Japan

underway, visitor arrivals dropped one-half of one percent to 3.9 million in 1980, but by 1984 the numbers rose inexorably again to 4.8 million. Waikiki's charms appeared almost recession-proof. Amid the drop and rise, no one seemed to notice that without the sizeable influx of Japanese visitors and money, Waikiki's visitor boom would have fizzled in the mid-1980's. Instead it expanded to yet another level. The state visitor count approached six million in 1988. Just across Waikiki's Ala Wai Canal, a Japanese college opened.

became a common sight. Wealthy Japanese bought homes in Hawai'i, creating a breathtaking rise in real estate sales and prices, and some shocking new tax assessments. One defining tale of the era told of a Japanese millionaire, who cruised the streets in Kahala, just beyond Diamond Head. When he saw a house he liked, his chauffeur would run up to the door and offer a briefcase full of cash on the spot, sometimes a million dollars or more.

When the Japanese bubble economy burst in the early 1990's, and California struggled to escape a recession, Hawai'i's visitor numbers and income finally slowed, stabilized, and sank. Waikiki, the reliable goose that laid the golden egg, now acknowledged that egg production was slipping. Conditioned by decades of rapid growth, many of Waikiki's business people wondered what stable visitor numbers would mean. In late 1999, the president of a major island bank said, "The good old days are gone. From here on we'll have to live in the real world." [27]

It is a bit breathtaking to review what Waikiki produced for the state of Hawai'i during its boom years. Rising visitor income had fueled the growth of Hawai'i's economy for two generations, as

was for them. Since statehood tiny Waikiki had generated staggering economic numbers — receiving around 100,000,000 visitors and producing some 130 billion dollars of income. Out of that economic flow had come over a billion and a half meals served, millions of cars rented and photos taken, and untold numbers of mu'umu'us sold and pineapples shipped. Visitor industry income had translated into a more prosperous Hawaiian society. Whatever people's nostalgia for the beach before the postwar visitor boom, or their concerns about how Waikiki's resources had been used, Waikiki had allowed Hawai'i's residents to realize their economic dreams.

construction, businesses, government, schools, and infrastructure improvements scrambled to keep pace with visitor and population growth. Visitor trade in the mid-1980's represented roughly 34% of everything that Hawai'i produced. [28] But with more visitors flocking to the outer islands, Waikiki now produced only six dollars out of ten, down from the nine dollars out of ten when jets first arrived.

University of Hawai'i historian Richard Rapson suggests that much of history lies in discovering what everyday people in a given era considered their dream of the good life, and how attainable it

Kamehameha the Great's sleepy Waikiki had evolved into the most valuable economic asset in the state, and one of the most sought after places in the world. Over the years there had been conference after conference on Waikiki's future and needs. Now in hopes of drawing more visitors, the state built a multi-million dollar convention center to anchor the Ewa end of Waikiki. When thirty thousand members of the American Dental Association arrived for the first major convention at the new facility in October of 1999, there were toothy smiles all over Waikiki.

Photographed from The Waikiki Landmark.

CHAPTER

Waikiki: Such Stuff As Dreams Are Made On

We learn from history that we do not learn from history.
George Friedrich Wilhelm Hegel

So there you have a history of Waikiki — paradise past and present. As the new century begins, some 6.8 million visitors a year come to Hawai'i, about half of them to Waikiki. After a twenty-year building moratorium, the urban landscape of Waikiki has subtlety begun to shift. Planners and entrepreneurs envision new attractions, more open space and greenery, a wider beach, and a reemphasis on the Hawaiian character that makes Waikiki unique.

Travel gurus predict a doubling of worldwide tourism over the next quarter of a century, but just what that may mean for Waikiki

One Waikiki is too tall, too urban, too crowded, and too commercial, a once sacred place out of touch with its Hawaiian roots. This Waikiki has all the problems of any crowded urban community. Some people long to see it return to the nostalgic past, when a slower pace and a simpler life gave the beach the feeling of a small town. They prefer a Waikiki of the 1940's or 50's. But a Waikiki with far fewer visitors and buildings would mean a major economic setback for the state, and no one knows how to get the clock in paradise to run backwards. So the present Waikiki, a successful urban visitor

and its physical limits remains a mystery. The Union of Concerned Scientists forecasts that global warming in the 21st century may raise sea levels about four inches a decade, suggesting that Waikiki might resemble Venice sixty to eighty years into the century. Those staring into crystal balls scratch their heads in puzzlement. Global warming, a rising interest in Hawaiian sovereignty, tidal shifts in global trade — what these and a dozen other possible influences have in store for Waikiki remains uncertain.

If you've spent much time here, you have probably come to realize that there are many Waikikis.

destination, is a place looking for an agreeable balance of business on one hand, and thriving Hawaiian culture, environmental sustainability, and beauty on the other.

In another Waikiki, Hawaiian tradition flows from the ancient past. Here spirits (*amakua*) appear in plants, creatures, and the many faces of nature. For many Hawaiians — in spirit or by blood — Waikiki remains a place of special *mana*, power. The influence of the Kamehamehas, Queen Emma, King Kalakaua, Princess Bernice Pauahi Bishop, and Princess Ka'iulani reawakens every day in the Hawaiians who perform music and dance telling the stories of Hawaiian culture.

THE FACE

In the half century following World War II, architects transformed the sleepy, low rise character of Waikiki into a densely populated, high rise cityscape — hotels, restaurants, condominiums, and retail businesses that accommodated the rising tide of visitors. These architects shaped millions of visitors' dreams of Waikiki, as well as how local people felt about Waikiki, a place where almost every resident had childhood experiences and memories.

The famed Waikikian, designed by Pete Wimberly shortly after its opening, circa 1958

The Hawai'i Convention Center, designed by Wimberly Allison Tong & Goo architects.

O F   W A I K I K I

As tall buildings inexorably replaced rows of one- and two-story homes and apartments that had defined the "Waikiki Jungle," the easy viewplanes of the area were lost, along with the mountains, ocean, and horizon. The feeling of small-town Waikiki began to disappear.

A few architects created places that became integral parts of Waikiki. They captured Polynesian influences and an informal, tropical feeling. Perhaps the best of these architectural talents was Pete Wimberly, who, incorporated natural materials indigenous to the tropics, and a remarkable sense of place to give us: the original International Market Place built around one of Waikiki's oldest banyan trees; Canlis Restaurant, the award-winning Waikikian Hotel and its famed Tahitian Lanai (once the watering hole for every famous Hawaiian entertainer and dancer from Honolulu to Papeete) and a host of other Waikiki landmarks, large and small. Faced with the usual pressures to make maximum use of land, Wimberly maintained a sensitivity to local environment, to whatever extent he could.

Contemporary Waikiki searches for its roots at the threshold of the 21st century. As acknowledgment of a rich historic past and an impetus for renewal grows, the next generation of architects and builders provide us glimpses of what may come, as Waikiki is once again redefined. Like their predecessors — Wimberly, Ossipoff and perhaps the greatest influence in Pacific architecture, C.W. Dickey, they will leave behind them a standard to shoot for, in environments we can sustain.

Duty Free Shoppers Galleria in Waikiki.

Left: "Nike Town," Honu Group. Above: a Jean Charlot mural at the First Hawaiian Bank in Waikiki.

119

Waikiki also remains one of the premier surfing beaches in the world. Unlike the North Shore's winter monsters, her gentle waves offer an easy challenge and a long ride. Beachboys still teach visitors how to swim, surf, and kick back, the same way John D. Kaupiko, and Joe Akana and the other old timers did years ago. At hotel luaus, Hawaiians pull the pig out of the *imu*, and Hawaiians make *poi* — the same foods they ate a thousand years ago. Someone still explains the delicate grace of the hula, someone sings in a soaring Hawaiian falsetto, and Hawaiian musicians play romantic songs that haunt your dreams — and your memories, of Waikiki.

away into the deeper blue of the endless Pacific. The cast of reef characters ranges from Moorish Idols and bright parrotfish to the tongue-tangling *Humuhumunukunukuapua'a*. Once you enter it with mask and snorkel, it is a world you cannot forget.

Since antiquity, islands have offered continent-bound people places where routine formalities of their own societies disappear. As modern cities of the world grow more crowded, the utopian possibilities of life on a tropic island become attractive. Waikiki has welcomed those bearing dreams of paradise, and here along the beach they have escaped the work-weary world to rest, heal, and ignore the relentless

Harry Robello and Squeeze Kamana, Jr.

For many, Waikiki is simply the warm, clear surf rolling at the shore, a leisurely nap, a family picnic, and a friendly climate that makes nature available year round. Waikiki is the play of light on monkeypod and shower trees, a jog around the green stretches of Kapi'olani Park, a swim, a glass of wine as sunset paints the horizon, and later, a moonlit walk in the shadow of Diamond Head.

From the ocean's edge, sand stretches toward the reef and falls

passage of time. They have played, loved, and reflected upon their dreams, for that is the message of Waikiki.

Hawaiian culture traditionally has observed a season called *makahiki*, a three month period of games and celebrations. Modern Waikiki carries part of this spirit. Along this beach you can find a microcosm of what people the world over long for, the chance to relax and find happiness.

Why Waikiki? Perhaps because here you find yourself living in the moment. Here the universal language of life can speak irresistibly — in the warmth of the sand beneath your feet, the roll of the sea, the cast of sunlight, and the quiet rustle of palm fronds stirring in trade winds. Beauty here can persuade you in wordless ways, allowing you to find your own paradise within.

For centuries Waikiki's mana, aloha, and enduring allure have beckoned and seduced countless dreamers, each drawn to this distant shore by the possibility of paradise. And the next chapter of this story belongs to you, in Waikiki . . . in the wake of dreams.

EDGY LEE

EDGY LEE is a fifth generation, Hawai'i-born writer, artist and award-winning documentary filmmaker. She has produced records, from the Wailers to His Holiness the 14th Dalai Lama. Her films have received international awards and acclaim; among them, *Paniolo O Hawai'i ~ Cowboys of the Far West* (a tribute to Hawai'i's cowboys who rode the ranges decades before their brethren in the American West), *Papakolea, Story of Hawaiian Land*, and *Waikiki, In the Wake of Dreams* — the film that accompanies this book.

Edgy claims that it was not just the promise of big fun that lured her into moving back home, but "a history that needed telling in the only place on Earth where restaurants offer you a choice of three starches..."

PAUL BERRY

PAUL BERRY, alias "Doc," has been a teacher/writer/editor/video producer in Honolulu for over three decades. The book and film *Waikiki — In the Wake of Dreams* represent his latest writing collaborations with Edgy Lee, with whom he also co-wrote the award winning film, *Paniolo O Hawaii - Cowboys of the Far West*.

Berry's recent works include a book on Hawai'i's environment, and two books with photographer Chris Rainier on ancient cultures and modern pressures for change.

MICHEL V.M. LÊ

MICHEL V.M. LÊ is an award-winning designer and graphic designer. Even as a small child, Michel knew he'd be an artist. He is both classically trained and self-taught, attending both La Sorbonne and Les Ateliers School of Design in Paris, but leaving to concentrate on his own style.

Michel has worked in ad agencies and design studios in Paris, London and New York, in the latter designing corporate materials, advertising, posters, and point-of-purchase materials for Marvel Comics. He has created Honolulu Magazine's popular look since April of 1998.

Right: From the documentary film *Waikiki, In the Wake of Dreams.*
Row 1: Director Edgy Lee interviewing Laura Guerrero & Nip Akona; Kamaka Clark Miyamoto; Sam Kapu.
Row 2: Tom Moffatt; Haumea Heibenstreit, beachboys at Steamboat Mokuahi's funeral.
Row 3: Boyce Rodrigues & Robert Cazimero; Don Ho; narrator Keaola Beamer, Sr.
Row 4: Benny Kalama; Henry Ayau; Jerry Byrd.
Row 5: Edgy & cameraman George Dvorsky; George Kanahele; Larry Mehau & Eddie Sherman.

Art & Photo Credits

WAIKIKI,
IN THE WAKE OF DREAMS

HP = Honolulu Publishing
HAA = Honolulu Academy of Arts
BPBM = B.P. Bishop Museum
HSA = Hawai'i State Archives
HMC = Hawai'i Maritime Center
FW = FilmWorks, Ltd.
GT = Grady Timmons
WATG = Wimberly Allison Tong &
Goo architects
MS = MacKinnon Simpson

4: courtesy HP
6: photo M.V.M. Lê
8: courtesy HP
10: *Men in Fruitladen Canoe*, Arman
T. Manookian ca. 1929; courtesy of
Mr. and Mrs. C. F. Damon, Jr., photo
courtesy of HAA
12-13: photo: O. Koning/FW
14: left & middle: photos:
O. Koning
15: left & middle: photos
O. Koning/FW; right: photo:
O. Koning
16-17: *Diamond Head*, ca. 1858,
painting by P. Emmert, courtesy
HAA; inset: photo: M.V.M. Lê
18-19: *Lily Pond and Coconut
Grove, Waikiki*, painting by H. W.
Kelley, courtesy BPBM
20: top: photo: O. Koning; bottom:
The Discovery of Oahu by Herb
Kawainui Kane, Collection of The
Outrigger Waikiki Hotel Coutesy of
the artist
21: left: courtesy MS; bottom: courtesy HP
22: bottom right: courtesy HP
23: left: *Kamehameha landing at
Waikiki* by Herb Kawainui Kane
Collection of Arthur Y. Wong
Coutesy of the artist; right &

background: courtesy HP
24: *Honolulu Harbor*, 1850 by
Peter Hurd, courtesy Amfac/JMB
Hawaii, L.L.C.
25: *Honolulu Harbor*, late 1880,
courtesy HSA
26: top right: photo: O. Koning/FW
27: top left: *The Sperm Whale in a
flurry*, litho. By N. Currier, courtesy
Crazy Shirts; top right: courtesy
HMC
29: top: courtesy HP; bottom:
Natives bathing in the surf, sketch
by J. Charlton, 1875, courtesy MS
30-31: *Honolulu from the anchorage outside the reef, island of
Wohahu, Sandwich Islands*, anon,
1834, courtesy BPBM
32-34: courtesy HP
35: photos: M.V.M. Lê
36: left courtesy E. Lee, right courtesy J. Cox Collection
37: top left: courtesy HP; top right
& bottom spread: courtesy BPBM
38: courtesy HP
39: left: courtesy HP; right courtesy
HSA
40: left: courtesy HSA; right:
courtesy HPBM
41: courtesy HSA; insert: photo:
O. Koning/FW
42: bottom left: *Kolomana:
Hawaiian Troubadour*, 1898, by
H. Vos, courtesy Proctor Stafford &
the Honolulu Academy of Arts; top
right: photo: O. Koning/ FW;
bottom right: photo: M.V.M. Lê
43: top right: photo: M.V.M. Lê;
bottom left/right: courtesy HP
44: top & second from top: BPBM,
others: courtesy HP
45: courtesy HP
46: left: courtesy J.Williams/BPBM;
right: courtesy HSA
47: top: courtesy HSA; bottom:
courtesy BPBM

48: courtesy HP
49: top & middle: courtesy BPBM;
bottom & insert: courtesy HP
50: left: photo: O. Koning; right:
courtesy HP
51: courtesy HP
52-53: photo: G. Wilcox, courtesy GT
54: top left & right: courtesy HP;
bottom: courtesy RVDC
55: top: courtesy M. Lyons; bottom:
courtesy BPBM
56: courtesy HSA
57: photos: O. Koning/FilmWorks;
left: courtesy BPBM
58: courtesy HP
59: top left: courtesy HP; others:
courtesy BPMP
60: left: courtesy HP; right:
courtesy BPBM
61: courtesy BPBM
62: left: courtesy BPBM; top &
bottom right: courtesy HP
63: middle & right: courtesy HP;
64: top: courtesy BPBM; bottom:
Surfriders by C.W. Barlett,
courtesy HP
65: top left, middle & bottom:
courtesy HP; top right: courtesy
BPBM
66: Matson menu, by E. Savage,
courtesy HP
67: top: photo: M.V.M. Lê; bottom:
middle & bottom: courtesy HP
68: top left: courtesy HSA; bottom:
courtesy HP; right: photo:
O. Koning/FW
69: courtesy HP
70: courtesy HP
71: left: courtesy BPBM
72-73: Matson menu, by Eugene
Savage, courtesy Matson
Navigation Company
74: top right: photo: O. Koning/
FW; others: courtesy HP
75: top & middle: courtesy HSA;
bottom: courtesy Oscar deWilde

76: left: HSA; right: photo: J.M.
Takatsugi, courtesy GT
77: courtesy HP; right: courtesy
BPBM
78: center photo: C. Lambert;
courtesy GT, bottom right:
courtesy GT
79: (top) courtesy Akana family
80: top left: photo: O.Koning/FW;
middle: photo: M.V.M. Lê; bottom:
courtesy HP; top right: courtesy
BPBM
81: bottom left: courtesy HSA;
others: courtesy HP
82: center: courtesy HP; bottom
left: photo M.V.M. Lê; top right:
photo: O. Koning/FW
83: bottom left: courtesy HSA; top
left: FilmWorks, top & bottom
right: courtesy HP
84: top: courtesy GT; bottom:
photo C. Lambert, courtesy GT
85: courtesy GT
86: top: courtesy GT; bottom:
courtesy HP
87: bottom left to right:
courtesy HP
88-89: courtesy BPBM
90: top: courtesy BPBM; bottom:
courtesy HP
91: top & bottom right: courtesy
HP, left courtesy J. Cox Collection
92: left: courtesy HP, right:
courtesy FW
93-95: courtesy HP
96-97: photos: O. Koning/FW
98: courtesy HP
99: top: courtesy HP; middle &
bottom: photo: O. Koning/FW
100: left: courtesy HP; top right:
courtesy BPBM; bottom right:
courtesy HP
101: top left: courtesy HP; middle
& bottom left: courtesy HP; top
right: courtesy MS
102: top left: photo: O. Koning/

FW; middle & bottom right:
courtesy HP
103: left: courtesy HP; right:
courtesy HP
104: top left: courtesy MS; top
right: courtesy HP; bottom left and
right: courtesy E. Rampell/L. Reyes
105: courtesy HP
106: left & top right: courtesy HP;
bottom right: photo: O. Koning/
FilmWorks
107: left background: courtesy
GT; Duke's statue: HVCB; top left
& center: courtesy HP; all others:
courtesy GT
108: top left, center left: courtesy
HP; right: photo Terry Luke,
private collection; bottom left:
courtesy HVCB; center right:
photo: O. Koning
109: top row from left: HVCB;
photo: O. Koning; photo:
O. Koning; courtesy HVCB;
bottom row: courtesy HP
110: courtesy H. Bauer
111: left & middle: photo: O.
Koning; right: courtesy HVCB
112: left: courtesy HVCB;
center: Preferred Stock; right:
photo: O. Koning; spread:
photo: O. Koning/FW
113: left & center: photo:
O. Koning; right: courtesy HVCB
114-115: photo: O. Koning
116-117: photos: O. Koning
118: photo: O. Koning/WATG
architects; inset: WATG architects
119: left: courtesy DFS Galleria;
middle & right: photos: O. Koning/
FW
120: left: J. Wellner/FW, middle &
right: O. Koning/WATG architects
121: photo: O. Koning/FW

WAIKIKI,
MAGIC BESIDE THE SEA

CHAPTER 1. MAGIC BESIDE THE SEA

*1 Ikuo Watanabe. Will Diamond Head Ever Erupt, monograph
2 Watanabe

CHAPTER 2. ANCIENT WAIKIKI

1 George Kanahele. *Waikiki; 100 BC to 1900 AD, An Untold Story.* pg. 62-64
2 Abraham Fornander. *Hawaiian Antiquities and Folklore.* vol. V. number 1. pg. 30-31
3 Kanahele. pg.62-64
4 Masakazu Ejiri. The Development of Waikiki. 1900-1949: The Formative Period of An American Resort Paradise. pg. 75
5 Abraham Fornander. *Ancient History of the Hawaiian People to the Times of Kamehameha I;* L.J Crampon. *Hawaii's Visitor Industry: Its Growth and Development,* Footnotes to Chapter II. pg. 292-293
6 William Ellis. *Polynesian Researches.* pg. 437-439
7 R. M. Daggett. "Introduction." *The Legends and Myths of Hawaii;* by King David Kalakaua. pg. 25. and Herb Kawainui Kane. *Voyagers,* pg. 73-76
8 H.J. Bartels. Tales of the Ala Wai Watershed. monograph
9 Ijiri. pg.24
10 David Malo. *Hawaiian Antiquities.* pg 221; John Papa I'i, *Fragments of History.* pg 68-69; Ellis. pg. 197-200; *Paradise of the Pacific.* October. 1893. pg.147
11 Samuel Kamakau. *Ruling Chiefs of Hawaii.* pg. 193
12 John B. Whitman. *An Account of the Sandwich Islands: 1813-1815.* pg. 70
13 *Paradise of the Pacific,* November. 1893. pg. 164
14 Kamakau. pg. 193; and *Encounters With Paradise,* David W. Forbes. pg. 64
15 L.J. Crampon. *Hawaii's Visitor Industry, Its Growth and Development,* Appendix 3. University of Hawaii School of Travel Industry Management. 1976. Unpublished Manuscript; and Hiram Bingham, *A Residence of Twenty-one Years in the Sandwich Islands.*
16 Kamakau. pg. 304

17 C.S. Stewart. *Journal of a Residence in the Sandwich Islands.* pg. 157
18 Kamakau. pg. 304
19 Walter Judd, *Hawaii Joins the World,* pg. 69
20 Kamakau. pg. 304
21 Kamakau. pg. 290
22 Crampon. pg. 60
23 Crampon. pg. 62
24 Stewart. pg. 135
25 Sybil Bingham. Letter. Mar 31,1820
26 Chester Smith Lyman. *The Hawaiian Journals of Chester Smith Lyman,* May 15. 1846- June 3. 1847

CHAPTER 3. SHAPING THE DREAM: 1848-1901

1 Mark Twain. *Letter to The Sacramento Union.* March, 1866
2 Mark Twain. *Roughing It,* pg. 455
3 Isabella Bird. *Six Months in The Sandwich Islands,* Letter. January 26. 1873.
4 Twain. *Roughing It,* pg. 477
5 Twain. *Roughing It,* pg. 455
6 Twain. *Roughing It,* pg. 462-63
7 Mark Twain. *Letter to The Sacramento Union.* April 24. 1866
8 Twain. unfinished novel
9 Bird. *A Chapter on Hawaiian Affairs.*
10 Bird. *Letter,* March 23. 1873.
11 Bird. *Letter,* March 23. 1873.
12 Crampon. appendix
13 *Pacific Commercial Advertiser,* Oct. 17. 1861
14 Thomas Thrum. *Hawaiian Annual,* 1881. pg. 40
15 Twain. *Letters,* pg. 132
16 Queen Emma. *Hawaiian Journal of History;* vol. 22. pg. 105
17 George Kanahele. *Waikiki 100 B.C. to 1900 A.D. An Untold Story;* pg.138
18 Agnes Quigg. *Hawaiian Journal of History;* vol. 22. 1988. pg. 170
19 Ijiri. pg. 85-88, and Harry T. Mills. "Area has had Colorful History from Days when Ostriches Roamed the Red Dirt Hills." Sept. 4. 1939, *Hawaiian Journal of History;* Vol 10
20 Jim Beloff. *The Ukulele: A Visual History,* pg. 11-18
21 Ken Kapua. *The Hawaiian Steel Guitar, and its Great Hawaiian Musicians,* pg. 2
22 Robert C. Schmitt, *Firsts and Almost Firsts in Hawaii,* pg. 58-9
23 Crampon. pg. 62
24 Robert Louis Stevenson. *Travels in Hawaii,* (1889. Kanahele. pg.146)
25 Crampon. pg. 193
26 Helena G. Allen. *Kalakaua, Renaissance King,* pg. 229

27 Crampon. pg. 221
28 Nick Carroll. "Duke Kahanamoku." *Surfer Magazine 25th Anniversary Edition,* pg. 1
29 Marilyn Stassen-McLaughlin. "Ainahau: A Paradise for a Princess." *Honolulu Magazine,* November. 1986. pg. 126
30 *Paradise of the Pacific,* 1893. October. pg. 147; Ijiri. pg. 123-24
31 Karl Kase. *Paradise of the Pacific,* August. 1894. pg. 104
32 Lemon "Rusty" Holt. *Waikiki, 1900-1985: Oral Histories, vol. II,* pg. 801-2
33. Mark Twain. unfinished novel

CHAPTER 4. COMING OF AGE

1 *Paradise of the Pacific,* September. 1898. pg. 129-30
2 Jack London, *The Cruise of the Snark,* 1911
3 Grady Timmons. *Waikiki Beachboy.* pg. 28. and "The Hollingers of Waikiki." Albert Summerall. monograph
4 Nick Carroll. "Duke Kahanamoku." *Surfing Magazine Twenty-fifth Anniversary Edition,* unpaginated
5 Fred Hemmings, *The Soul of Surfing Is Hawaiian.* pg. 16
6 Earl Vida. *Waikiki, 1900-1985: Oral History, vol II,* pg. 604-5
7 Dave Parmenter. "Duke Kahanamoku." *Surfer 40th Anniversary Edition,* pg. 194-199; Carroll: interview with Kamaka Miyamoto
8 Parmenter. pg. 199
9 Don Hibbard and David Franzen, *The View From Diamond Head,* pg. 83
10 Beloff. pg. 17 18: Crampon. pg. 234-236
11 Beloff. pg. 19-31
12 Swing Rhythm. Ray Smeck plays solo ukulele. Tiger Rag." Harry Wright film collection. Library of Congress
13 George Kanahele. *Hawaiian Music and Musicians,* pg. 68-70, 267-269
14 Kanahele. *Hawaiian Music and Musicians,* pg. 143-146
15 Carroll.
16 Parmenter. pg. 194-199; Carroll: Kamaka Miyamoto, interview
17 Parmenter. pg.199, and Carroll.
18 Sadao Hikida, *Waikiki, 1900-1985: Oral Histories, vol. II,* pg. 968
19 Earl Vida. *Waikiki, 1900-1985: Oral Histories, vol II,* pg. 558, 585-588

20 Rebecca Kapule. *Waikiki, 1900-1985: Oral Histories, vol. I,* pg. 393
21 Esther Jackson Bader. *Waikiki, 1900-1985: Oral Histories, vol I,* pg. 427
22 Fred Paoa. *Waikiki, 1900-1985: Oral Histories, vol. II,* pg. 573
23 Joe Akana. *Waikiki, 1900-1985: Oral Histories, vol. I,* pg. 42
24 Lemon Rusty Holt. *Waikiki, 1900-1985: Oral Histories, vol.II,* pg. 779
25 Masakazu Ejiri. *The Development of Waikiki, 1900-1949,* pg. 242-250. preceding two paragraphs
26 Ejiri. pg. 248. and Ed Coll and Carol Bain. *Taking Waikiki, From Self-Sufficiency to Dependency.* pg.16
27 Vida. pg. 586-7
28 Crampon. Statistical Appendix
29 Crampon. pg. 261
30 Crampon. pg. 261-262
31 Robert C. Schmitt. *Firsts and Almost Firsts in Hawaii,* pg. 50-52; Crampon. pg. 273; Dole Cup Race. Movietone News, 1927. National Archives
32 Crampon. pg. 272-274; Movietone News
33 Matson Navigation Company. *Matson, A Century of Service,* pg. 73
34 Louis Kahanamoku. s pg.877
35 Crampon. pg. 241
36 Crampon. pg 242
37 Peter Docker and Bob Thomas. *The Massie Case,* passim

CHAPTER 5 THE GOLDEN ERA

1 Jerry Byrd. interview
2 Don Blanding. *Vagabonds House,* pg. 104
3 Fred Paoa. *Waikiki, 1900-1985: Oral Histories, vol. II,* pg. 557-559
4 Joe Akana. *Waikiki, 1900-1985: Oral Histories, vol. I,* pg. 18 & 555
5 Hemmings. pg. 16
6 Crampon. pg. 284
7 Robert Pfeiffer. interview
8 Benny Kalama. interview
9 Sen. Dan Inouye. interview

CHAPTER 6 WAIKIKI GOES TO WAR

1 Gwenfread Allen, *Hawaii's War Years,* passim
2 Hawaii Judiciary Martial Law Exhibit. 1999
3 Sen. Dan Inouye. interview
4 Ronald Takaki. *Strangers From a Different Shore: A History of Asian Americans,* pp. 380-384
5 Takaki. pg. 390. preceding paragraph
6 Hawaii Judiciary Martial Law Exhibit
7 Beth Bailey and David Farber. *The*

First Strange Place, pg. 98; Gwenfread Allen. *Hawaii's War Years,* pg. 354
8 Benny. Kalama. interview
9 Bailey and Farber. pg. 126-7
10 *Honolulu Advertiser,* Sept. 22. 1944. pg 18
11 Allen. pg. 259
12 Allen. pg. 260

CHAPTER 7. ANATOMY OF A BOOM

1 Sadao Hikida. *Waikiki, 1900-1985: Oral Histories,* pg. 974
2 Crampon. pg.288 and Statistical Appendix
3 Beloff. pg. 65
4 Arthur Lyman. interview
5 Crampon. Statistical Appendix
6 John McDermott. *Kelleys of the Outrigger,* pg. 50
7 Crampon. Statistical Index
8 Duane Preble and Tony Hodges. interviews
9 The Honorable Robert Klein. interview
10 Warren Nishimoto. *Waikiki, 1900-1985: Oral Histories, vol. II,* Appendix. pg. A-19
11 Passenger Statistics of Hawaii. Statistical Report 75. Department of Planning and Economic Development. and Eleanor Nordyke. *The Peopling of Hawaii,* Table 5.2
12 Eddie Sherman. interview
13 Don Ho. interview
14 Don Ho. interview
15 Eddie Sherman. interview
16 Larry Mehau. interview
17 Nordyke. Table 5-2
18 Nordyke. pg.144-147
19 Nordyke. pg. 134-166
20 Appendix. *Waikiki, 1900-1985: Oral Histories, vol. II* pg. 39
21 Andrew Gomes. "DFS Investing in Waikiki." *Honolulu Advertiser,* Sept. 25. 1999
22 Nordyke. pg. 134
23 John Griffin. *Honolulu Advertiser,* June 21. 1981; Nordyke. pg. 150
24 *Waikiki, 1900-1985, Oral Histories,* Appendix pg 43; Nordyke pg.150
25 *Waikiki: Hawaii's Premier Visitor Attraction,* Office of Planning. Department of Business. Economic Development and Tourism. State of Hawaii. 1998. pg. 6
26 *Waikiki, 1900-1985, Oral Histories, vol. II,* Appendix
27 Channel 4. KHON Newscast. September 5. 1999
28 Nordyke. pg. 145

Bibliography

Interviews and Conversations

Nip Akona, Henry Ayau, Keola Beamer, Manu Boyd, Jerry Byrd, Kalu Cummings, Laura Guerrero, Don Ho, Tony Hodges, Senator Daniel Inouye, Dr. George Kanahele, Rebecca Kapule, Benny Kalama, The Honorable Robert Klein, Arthur Lyman, Larry Mehau, Kamaka Miyamoto, Robert Pfeiffer, Boyce Rodrigues, Eddie Sherman, Dr. Duane Preble.

Bibliography

Akana, Joe. *Waikiki, 1900-1985: Oral Histories vol. 1*. University of Hawaii Press, 1985.

Allen, Gwenfread. *Hawaii's War Years*. University of Hawaii Press, 1950.

Allen, Helena G.. *Kalakaua, Renaissance Man*, Mutual Publishing, 1994.

Bader, Esther Jackson *Waikiki, 1900-1985: Oral Histories vol. 1*. University of Hawaii, 1985.

Bailey, Beth and David Farber. *The First Strange Place*, Johns Hopkins University Press, 1992.

Bartel, H.J.. Tales of the Ala Wai Watershed, monograph.

Beloff, Jim. *The Ukulele, A Visual History*, Miller Freeman Books, 1997.

Bingham, Hiram. "A Residence of Twenty-one Years in the Sandwich Islands," as found in Missionaries vs. Men-of-Warsmen, pg 47-50 in *A Hawaiian Reader*, A. Grove Day and Carl Stroven editors, Mutual Publishing, 1959.

Bingham, Sybil. 30 Mar 31,1820. HMCS Library.

Bird, Isabella. *Six Months in the Sandwich Islands*, Mutual Publishing, 1998.

Blanding, Don. *Vagabonds House*, Dodd, Mead, 1928.

Brown, DeSoto. *Hawaii Goes to War*, Editions Limited, 1989.

Campbell, Archibald. *Voyage Round the World, 1802-1812*, Topgallant Press.

Carroll, Nick. "Duke Kahanamoku: A Tribute to the Father of Modern Surfing," *Surfing Magazine; Twenty-fifth Anniversary Edition*. Surfing Magazine.

Chaplin, George and Glenn Paige, editors. *Hawaii 2000, Governors Conference on the Year 2000*, State of Hawaii, 1974.

Ed Coll and Carol Bain, *Taking Waikiki, From*

Self-Sufficiency to Dependency, Kauai Worldwide Communications, Inc.1994.

Crampon, L.J. *Hawaii's Visitor Industry; Its Growth and Development*, University of Hawaii School of Travel Industry and Management, unpublished manuscript.

Daggett, R.M., Introduction, *The Legends and Myths of Hawaii*, by King David Kalakaua, Mutual Publishing, 1990.

Docker, Peter and Bob Thomas, *The Massie Case*, Bantam, 1966.

Ejiri, Masakazu. The Development of Waikiki, 1900-1949: The Formative Period of An American Resort Paradise. University of Hawaii doctoral dissertation in American Studies.

Ellis, William. *Polynesian Researches*, Charles E. Tuttle Company, 1969.

Forbes, David W. *Encounters With Paradise, Views of Hawaii and Its People 1778-1941*, Honolulu Academy of Arts, 1992.

Fornander, Abraham. *Ancient History of the Hawaiian People to the Times of Kamehameha I*, Glen Grant, editor, Mutual Publishing, 1996.

Finney, Ben and James D. Houston, *Surfing: A History of the Ancient Hawaiian Sport*, Pomegranate Artbooks, 1996.

Furnas, J.C., *Anatomy of Paradise: Hawaii and the Islands of the South Seas*, William Sloane Associates, 1937.

Gomes, Andrew, *DFS Investing in Waikiki*, Honolulu Advertiser, Sept. 25, 1999.

Hemmings, Fred, *The Soul of Surfing Is Hawaiian*, Arts Enterprises, 1997.

Hawaii Judiciary Martial Law Exhibit, 1999.

Hibbard, Don and David Franzen, *The View From Diamond Head*, Editions Limited, 1986.

Hikida, Sadao. *Waikiki, 1900-1985, Oral Histories, vol. II*, University of Hawaii, 1985.

Honolulu Magazine, December, 1999.

Holman, Lucia Ruggles, April, 1820. Bishop Museum Press.

Holt, Lemon "Rusty," *Waikiki, 1900-1985, Oral Histories, vol. II*, University of Hawaii 1986.

Ii, John Papa. *Fragments of History*, Bishop Museum Press, 1993.

Jarves, James J. *History of the Sandwich Islands*, Tappan & Dennet, 1843.

Judd, Laura, Letter to Sybil Bingham, Sept.2, 1844. Bingham Family Papers, Box 3, MHML.

Judd, Walter. *Hawaii Joins the World*, Mutual Publishing, 1998.

Juvik, Sonia P. and James O., *Atlas of Hawaii*, Third Edition, University of Hawaii Press, 1998.

Kahanamoku, Louis.*Waikiki, 1900-1985, Oral Histories, vol. II*, University of Hawaii, 1985.

Kamakau, Samuel. *Ruling Chiefs of Hawaii*, Kamehameha Schools Press, 1992.

Kanahele, George. *Hawaiian Music and Musicians*, University of Hawaii Press, 1979.

Kanahele, George. *Restoring Hawaiianness To Waikiki*, Queen Emma Foundation, 1994.

Kanahele, George. *Waikiki 100 B.C. to 1900 A.D. An Untold Story*, Queen Emma Foundation, 1995.

Kane, Herb Kawainui. *Voyagers*, Whalesong, 1991.

Kapua, Ken. "Joseph Kekuku. Originator of the Hawaiian Guitar," in *The Hawaiian Steel Guitar, and its Great Hawaiian Musicians*, Lorene Ruymar, editor, Centerstream Publishing, 1996.

Kapule, Rebecca, *Waikiki, 1900-1985, Oral Histories, vol. I*, University of Hawaii, 1985.

Kase, Karl. *Paradise of the Pacific*, August, 1894.

Kuykendall, R.S. *The Hawaiian Kingdom, Volume 1: 1778-1854*, University of Hawaii Press, 1968.

London, Jack. "A Royal Sport: Surfing at Waikiki," *The Cruise of the Snark*, Macmillan, 1911.

Lyman, Chester Smith, *The Hawaiian Journals of Chester Smith Lyman*, May 15, 1846-June 3, 1847.

Malo, David. *Hawaiian Antiquities*, Moolelo Hawaii, Hawaiian Gazette Co. 1903.

McDermott, John W. *Kelleys of the Outrigger*, ORAFA Publishing, 1990.

Mills, Harry T. "Area Has Had Colorful History from Days when Ostriches Roamed the Red Dirt Hills" HA Sept. 4, 1939 *Hawaii Journal of History vol. 10*.

Native Hawaiian Data Book, 1998. Office of Hawaiian Affairs, State of Hawaii.

Nordyke, Eleanor, *The Peopling of Hawaii*, Second Edition, University of Hawaii Press, 1989.

Pacific Commercial Advertiser, Oct. 17, 1861.

Pacific Commercial Advertiser, Feb. 1, 1879.

Paoa, Fred. *Waikiki, 1900-1985, Oral Histories, vol. II*, University of Hawaii, 1985.

Paradise of the Pacific, October, 1893.

Paradise of the Pacific, September, 1898.

Parmenter, Dave. "The Twenty-Five Most Influential Surfers of the Century: 1900-1999,"

Surfer Magazine 40th Anniversary Issue.

Quigg, Agnes, *Hawaii Journal of History vol. 22*, 1988.

Ruymar, Lorene, *The Hawaiian Steel Guitar and Its Great Hawaiian Musicians*, Centerstream Publishing, 1996.

Rayson, Ann. *Modern Hawaiian History*, Bess Press, 1984.

Scott, E.B., *Saga of the Sandwich Islands*, Sierra Tahoe Publishing Company, 1968.

Schmitt, Robert C., *Firsts and Almost Firsts in Hawaii*, University of Hawaii Press, 1995.

Stassen-MacLaughlin, Marilyn, "Ainahau: A Paradise for a Princess, *Honolulu Magazine*, November, 1986.

Stevenson, Robert Louis, *Travels in Hawaii*, University of Hawaii Press, 1973.

Stewart, C.S. *Journal of a Residence in the Sandwich Islands*.

Stone, Scott, *Honolulu, Heart of Hawaii*, Continental Heritage Press, 1983.

Summerall, Albert, The Hollingers of Waikiki, monograph.

Swing Rhythm , Ray Smeck plays solo ukulele, Tiger Rag, Harry Wright Film Collection, Library of Congress.

Takaki, Ronald, *Strangers From a Different Shore: A History of Asian Americans*, Little Brown, 1989.

Taylor, Lois, *Honolulu Star-Bulletin*, May 10, 1981.

Thurston, Lorrin A.. *Memoirs of the Hawaiian Revolution*.

Thrum, Thomas. *Hawaiian Annual*, 1881.

Timmons, Grady, *Waikiki Beachboy*, Editions Limited, 1989.

Transpac Air Race of 1927, Movietone News, National Archives Film Division.

Twain, Mark, *Letters To The Sacramento Union*, 1866. http://www.tarleton.edu/~schmidt/sd

Twain, Mark, *Roughing It*, American Publishing Company, 1872, Hartford, Connecticut.

Vancouver, George, *Voyage of Discovery To the Pacific Ocean*, G.G.and J Robinson, 1798.

Vida, Earl. *Waikiki, 1900-1985, Oral Histories, vol. II*, University of Hawaii, 1985.

Whitman, John B.. *An Account of the Sandwich Islands: 1813-1815*, John Dominis Holt, editor, Topgallant Press, 1979.

Zambucka, Kristin. *Kalakaua, Hawaii's Last King*, Mana Publishing, 1983.